TOWERS & TURRETS OF EUROPE

Photography: Heinz Bronowski   *Text: Günter Meissner*

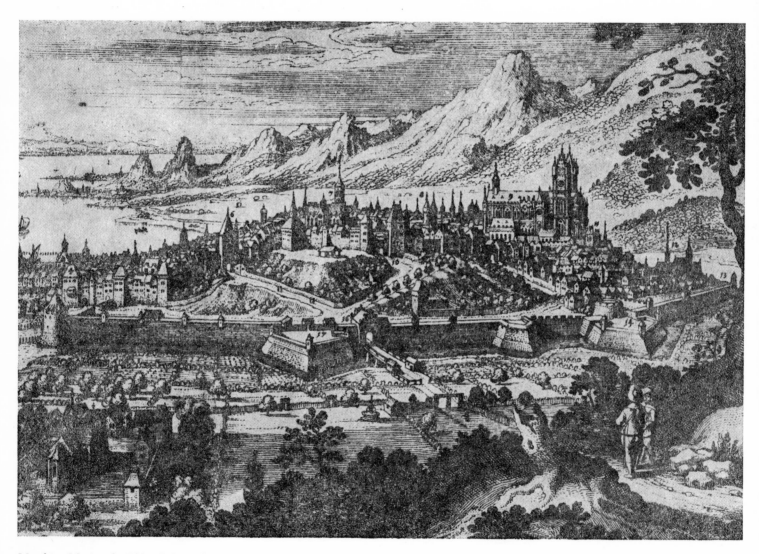

Matthäus Merian the Elder. "View of Geneva," 1644

TOWERS & TURRETS OF EUROPE

HART PUBLISHING COMPANY, INC.
NEW YORK CITY

TYPOGRAPHY AND DESIGN BY WALTER SCHILLER

COPYRIGHT © 1972 BY EDITION LEIPZIG
FIRST AMERICAN PUBLICATION 1974
ISBN NO. 08055-1124-5
PRINTED IN GERMANY (EAST)

CONTENTS

INTRODUCTION

Towers and gateways have always played a special part in architecture. Temples and churches, citadels, fortresses, castles, town halls, theaters, museums, sports stadiums—each emerged in a specific historical period and experienced a golden age. But the tower and, up to the last century, the gateway have continued to be vital parts of the architectural scene in each succeeding period. Their important basic functions have made them indispensable to society. The gateway in the city wall was an imposing entrance and, at the same time, a part of the city's system of defense, often in conjunction with towers. The tower is, thanks to its height, capable of performing a wide range of defense functions, such as observation, the transmission or reception of signals, and actual combat.

Since both gates and towers were community structures and were of a high architectonic, aesthetic, and emotional quality, they tended to transcend their actual purposes and become symbols for the people of the area. Right down to the present time, they have lost nothing of their fascination. What would Paris be without the Eiffel Tower, Berlin without the Brandenburg Gate, Moscow without the Spassky Tower, Prague without the Old Town Clock Tower? For people from other places, these kinds of structures are unmistakable symbols of the cities they grace, but to the city's natives they are old friends who are given affectionate nicknames. The Londoner has "Big Ben," the

Dutchman in Middelburg his "Long Jan," and the Viennese has "Old Steffel."

This book is a review of characteristic European towers, gateways, and arches. In the course of thousands of years, many generations have given testimony to their creative genius. Only a few of the names of the gate and tower builders have been handed down. Built by the common people—though all too often not in their interests—these structures underline the spirit of their time in their anonymity.

Our century no longer has any functional use for the majority of these gateways and towers. They have become monuments—meaningless, it would seem, apart from their place in the history of art. But this is not so, for the living elements, the principles of this heritage, almost imperceptibly continue to influence architecture today. True, the gateway has largely lost its original aesthetic and practical purpose, but the tower continues to flourish in a new form and, most important, in new dimensions. The tower makes us contemporaries with our forebears, unseparated by historical distance, witnesses of a momentous technical and artistic revolution. Mankind's ancient dream of building as high as the clouds, of conquering the sky—as expressed by the ill-fated Tower of Babel—is becoming reality. The highest towers have already reached heights of over 1,500 feet. Are there limits to the human spirit's need to climb higher and higher?

As far back as 5,000 years ago, still imbued with mystic ideas, man sought to assert himself with that legendary tower of Babylon. He had to fail. The low level of productivity in a slave-owning society would not permit the clouds to be reached, no matter how massive the use of manpower. Since then, according to the Bible, as the punishment of God there has been a "confusion of tongues."

Archaeological excavations have thrown light on the true background of the European tower. The ziggurat of Babylon, literally "the mountain of the gods," was a colossal brick edifice of terraced design, on the upper platform of which there was a temple dedicated to the supreme Babylonian god, Marduk. Erected about 2000 B. C., it was destroyed and rebuilt a number of times, the last time with a spiral ramp during the reign of Nebuchadnezzar, c. 600 B. C. The ziggurat finally ceased to exist after the conquest by the Persians; all that remains of it is a reconstructed drawing. The Babylonian ziggurat, which was not a tower but a forerunner of it, itself had predecessors, such as the ziggurat of Ur in Chaldea, and many other similar structures followed it.

At first sight, the stepped pyramids of Egypt would seem to be comparable to the ziggurats. However, since the pyramids were built upwards not to carry a crowning structure to the heavens but to conceal a burial chamber in the interior, the character of the tower is alien to them. Other early civilizations, such as those of ancient Mexico, also erected cult monuments of a stepped, terracelike form. Since the Mexican structures were a culturally unrelated development, it may be concluded simply that the piling up of a mass of material was, for all early civilizations, the obvious way of attaining a great height. Faith literally "moved mountains."

It was not until thousands of years later, in the feudal period, that the power of Christianity and the desire of the great towns to display their wealth led to the building of even higher structures, the Gothic towers.

These examples show that great importance must be attached to *ideas* as the driving force in the building of towers. The towers rose above the struggles of thousands of years as eternal symbols in stone, the concrete expression of the ideas of the time. Nevertheless, religious abstractions did not entirely conceal the highly temporal desire of the persons commissioning the works to display and consolidate their own power. (Shifting briefly to the present, it may also be said that even in this secular age, neither the 984-foot-high Eiffel Tower not the 1,250-foot-high Empire State Building—which is not a tower—can be explained simply by functional considerations. They are examples of the urge to make record-breaking achievements, of the triumph of engineers, and of the expression of economic prosperity. They also proclaim the development of the creative power of man.)

The symbolic meaning, which even in the earliest times was so obvious an element in the urge to build to the sky, is of course not the only root of the tower structure. The need to defend the settlements which were established about 10,000 years ago, when the tillers of the land and the herdsmen began to form communities with a fixed base, led to the construction of earthwork systems, and later, walls with towers and gates. The first great empires of the ancient Orient and Middle East protected themselves with mighty defensive works, of which only a few have survived.

The magnificent Ishtar Gate from the Late Babylonian Period (570 B.C.) is an instructive example. One has to imagine a circular wall of brick, lined with battlements and reinforced with slightly projecting towerlike structures—which soon became towers in the wall—at short distances from each other. They were not only higher and thicker than the parts in between but were also set forward, so that the attacks of the enemy could be more effectively opposed from the upper platforms, using arrows, spears, and stones. That part of the wall which was especially vulnerable, the gate, was usually flanked by towers in close proximity to each other which were higher than the wall and extended far in front of it.

Since that time, the tower and the gate became associated within the sphere of urban fortifications, even though they were so diverse in construction. The Ishtar Gate of Babylon can be considered an early form of the double-towered gate. It was not until the Middle Ages, with the introduction of firearms, that further developments took place in gate architecture, with the construction of barbicans and double-gates with the keep.

Naturally enough, the clear-cut function of the wall towers could not allow any odd or artistically significant shape. Simple, massive, and squat, seldom of very great height, they stood around the cities like a circle of stone custodians. Only the gateways allowed scope for rich decoration. Above and beyond their function of providing an entry (which could be barred) for thousands of people, it was precisely at this point of constant contact with the

Reconstruction of the ziggurat at Babylon

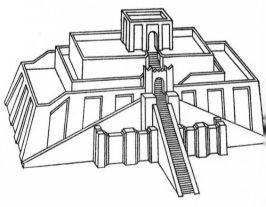

world outside that the need was felt to give an appropriate indication of the power and wealth of the city.

At the Ishtar Gate of Babylon, with the royal processional street, the visitor is impressed not only by the detail of the colored tiles used for decoration but also by the solemnity of the size and the severe rhythm of the ornamentation. This was an aura that would induce order, discipline, and even submission. The reliefs of lions, bulls, and dragons as symbols of royal majesty add to this markedly despotic consciousness of power.

Less militant but monumental in a similar way as the expression of an unshakable order was the design of the facades of the Egyptian temples. With their pylons, fortresslike gate towers flanking a comparatively narrow entrance (as illustrated by the temple of Horus at Edfu from the Late Period), the temples embodied in their stern majesty the unassailable, godlike power of the priests. Within the walls of their gigantic temple precincts, the priests were able to withstand not only rebellions of the people but even attacks by the pharaohs.

These strictly defined constructional types kept their position in the cult and fortress architecture of Egypt and the Middle East until new possibilities appeared in Europe with the emergence of the civilizations of Ancient Greece and Rome. However, the beginnings of European architecture were shaped by many influences from Egypt and the Middle East, for there was a common

social basis and the Mediterranean between them.

In Mycenae, the home of Agamemnon on the edge of Argolis, the ancestors of the Greeks built the walls of their citadel in about 1400 B.C., with stones of Cyclopean size. As in the Middle East but in more original fashion, these symbols of invincibility might bar the way for every adversary at the famous Lion Gate of Mycenae.

If the line of development is traced, it can be seen that gateways and towers were very much less important in Greek and Roman antiquity than in the civilizations which had gone before. Of course, these structures retained their defensive function. From the warlike Early Period of Rome, the double-towered Porta Augusta at Perugia (c. 1000 B.C.) is an instructive example, continuing the tradition of defense and display typified by the Ishtar Gate, yet emphasizing the military function.

Neither the Greek city-states nor the militant Roman Empire, whose legions in its golden age stood guard at places far from the mother country, attached any particular artistic importance to building towers and gateways. Moreover, the religious monument of antiquity was the temple, a building which with its horizontal and vertical elements formed a unity and, in the darkness of the "cella," a well-balanced abode for the sacred image of the god. But this god was not the forbidding and infallible authority of earlier times. The com-

munity of self-assured Greeks humanized the world of the gods and consequently built a house for them on human lines. The mighty tower surmounting a hill—indeed, even the tower itself as a transcendental symbol demanding humility—was therefore not represented in the religious structures of the Greeks.

One of the most beautiful gateways of that classical period is the Propylaea of the Acropolis at Athens, the work of the architect Mnesicles in the years 437—432 B.C. Inviting and not threatening, the stately entrance to the temple, flanked by two uncompleted wings blending harmoniously with the landscape, opened out onto the city. On public holidays, the free Greeks climbed the two flights of stairs to the Acropolis. What a contrast with the stern pylons of Egypt! It is not surprising that later periods, especially the Classical Period, found inspiration from this gateway, as demonstrated by the Brandenburg Gate in Berlin and the Propylaea at Munich, which were built in a similar style.

The brief golden age of Greek classicism was succeeded by the authoritarian Hellenistic empires, and the heritage of both periods passed to the Roman Empire in the last century B.C. While the Greek example continued to retain its validity, the desire of the newly emergent emperors for pomp and circumstance again stimulated the building of towers and gateways, although designs varied considerably, depending on the particular requirements.

One need very much in keeping with the character of the time was, for instance, the lighthouse. It took the place of the lantern on a column in the harbors of the Mediterranean during this period of extensive sea trade. There was no reason for the lighthouse to be more than about 120 feet in height, since this allowed it to be seen from a distance of more than 20 miles. Nevertheless, the lighthouse on the island of Pharos, one of the Seven Wonders of the World—which stood at the entrance to Alexandria, the most important port in the world at that time—was about 400 feet high. Its height and design, as indicated by the reconstructed drawing, go far beyond its actual purpose. Ptolemy II, who commissioned Sostratus to build the tower (completed in 280–279 B.C.), thus erected a monument which was visible to all in commemoration of his reign.

Too few have remained of these towers of antiquity which had a specific function and, it may be assumed, once existed in fairly large numbers. The "Tower of the Winds" in Athens, only 37 feet high and built at the time Greece was a Roman colony, was a clock tower, for instance. A sundial and a water clock told the time and a "weathercock," represented symbolically by the relief frieze of the gods of the winds, indicated the direction of the wind.

The nuraghe was a special form of tower, dating from a prehistoric tribal order and found until Roman times on Sardinia and Sicily in particular. The nuraghe was a bur-

ial and refuge tower, rather like a beehive in shape, whose massive walls were certainly capable of withstanding attack. This function was revived once more in the medieval keep which, as a freestanding and solidly built tower, represented the last refuge for the beaten defenders of a castle. Reference may also be made to the sepulcher tower, a monumental memorial containing only a sarcophagus. The early example of the Middle East was continued in the Etruscan and Roman cultures with a marked cult of the dead. The cylindrical was the most widely used of the many shapes of sepulcher towers. Some of these cylindrical towers were of enormous size and were turned into fortifications by later generations. The 1st-century tomb of Cae-

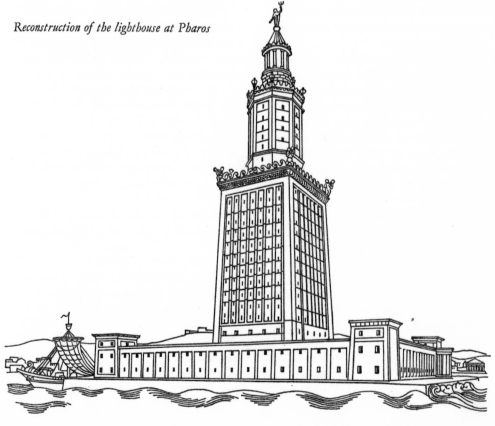

Reconstruction of the lighthouse at Pharos

cilia Metella by the Via Appia, or the mausoleum known as the Castel Sant'Angelo of the Emperor Hadrian in Rome, are evidence of this. The striking appearance of these free-standing, towerlike tombs is without doubt one reason why, at the beginning of Christian architecture in Italy, the clock tower stood in marked isolation at the side of the nave as a campanile, instead of being an element in an architectural group as in Northern Europe.

Yet before we venture the leap to a new epoch, there is still one outstanding type of structure from Roman antiquity which is often mistakenly considered as a gateway and deserves our attention—the triumphal arch. These triumphal arches originally consisted of a base on which there were arches, like a gateway in appearance and of very large size during the Imperial Period, carrying the statue or even the quadriga of the person honored. The triumphal arches were not designed as a way of access which could be barred—the essential characteristic of a gateway—but stood in an isolated position as a monument to be admired at a distance; the deeds recorded in lettering and relief illustrations could be read at close quarters.

The concept of the lofty and imposing monument of fame, alien to the Greek tradition but very much a part of the ancient Oriental civilizations, was thus revived in a new form in the authoritarian Roman state. The well-known examples of the arches of Severus and Constantine in Rome, to mention only two of the many which

could be named, utilize the very effective principle of a symmetrical layout in which the central arch, symbolizing the eminence of the person in question, is flanked by two smaller "satellite" arches. So impressive was the effect obtained that triumphal arches continued to be built from the Middle Ages to the 19th century. It is significant that absolutism and the ideas inspired by it in the last century provided a particularly good atmosphere for the triumphal arch. However, because these arches span great avenues, they have now become gateways through which automobile traffic can pass, as is the case with the Arc de Triomphe de l'Etoile in Paris.

The love of splendor and magnificence of the late Roman Imperial Period, was not at all the sign of increasing prosperity but rather the claim to power of an empire shaken by social struggles within and threatened by enemies without. Roman pomp was also reflected in its defensive structures, which had now become urgently necessary. Rome and Constantinople, the capitals of the two parts of the empire, were enclosed within mighty walls by Marcus Aurelius at the end of the 3rd century and by Theodosius at the end of the 4th. Every 25–30 yards, these walls were strengthened by towers. Mighty as these walls and gates were (as for example the Porta Nigra, built in the 3rd century in Trier in the style of a triumphal arch), a social order maintained and at the same time undermined by slaves had to yield.

In the storms of the Barbarian Invasions, the Western Roman Empire was the first to collapse, in the 5th century, while the Eastern Empire, threatened by Islam and long of a different character, was not conquered by the Turks until 1453. The fallen Empire passed on its crumbling stone edifices, including its fortifications, gateways, and towers, to the young peoples now emerging. Centuries were still to pass, however, before a new age of tower and gate architecture could dawn.

Nonetheless, this transitional period, which in Central and Western Europe came to an end with the founding of cities and the consolidation of the feudal order in the 11th century, was not entirely unproductive. The 6th-century clock towers of Ravenna or the gatehouse of the monastery at Lorsch—a jewel of the Carolingian architecture of the 8th century which consciously utilized the traditions of antiquity—are works indicative of change, with their signs of a nascent spirit of militant Christianity. This religion, at first only the creed of the oppressed, had already started to take root in slave-owning society.

On the basis of the traditions of antiquity, the characteristic types of church architecture gradually emerged: in the Greek Orthodox Byzantine sphere, primarily the central dome structure; in the Roman Catholic area, the basilica in the outline of the Latin cross, with a series of points at which towers could be built (especially at the west facade, the sides of the transept, and above the intersection). This desire for many towers in the Romanesque period and high towers in the Gothic—to mention a bit prematurely the two medieval styles in the period of the absolute supremacy of Christian dogma—cannot be explained by practical considerations. The possible necessity for defense, the custom of summoning the congregation by tolling a bell from an elevated position, the technical advantage of a spiral staircase for bringing up material— none of these justify the importance attached to towers in ecclesiastical architecture in Western and Central Europe. Historical perspective provides the explanation.

Towers are symbols in stone, proclaiming the supremacy of ideas which, in turn, support the claim to specific economic, social, and political power of the ruling class. In the Middle Ages, the number, ornateness, or height of towers was the outward sign of the omnipotence of God and, concomitantly, of his representatives on Earth, who demanded Christian humility from the common people.

It was therefore not mere chance that the soaring towers of the religious structures dominated the silhouette of the medieval community, and not mere chance that reformist and democratic currents within the Church itself led to a reduction of the number of towers from the 12th century on. As time passed, the development of bourgeois self-assurance and humanism increasingly rejected the tower as a religious symbol. The fact that in the Gothic Period especially a great number of church towers in the cities were built to very great heights and in a very elaborate manner indicates that structures such as these were a welcome opportunity for the people to demonstrate the prosperity of their cities, a prosperity which was essentially worldly.

Following this general introduction, no more than an impression can be given of the major types of church tower in Europe. By the end of Classical Antiquity, in the Early Christian era, the outstanding feature of medieval Italian tower structures had already appeared. This was the campanile, a free-standing bell tower. At the beginning of the 6th century, as shown by the example of San Apollinare Nuovo in Ravenna, the campanile was a simple, uncomplicated cylindrical structure. In later times, the tower was often of an elaborate design (Pisa, Siena) but, in contrast to the Gothic Tower, never lost its clear silhouette or its marked horizontal rhythm. This and the fact that the campanile at the side of the basilica in most cases remained the only church tower symbol is explained by the traditions of antiquity, which continued to influence Italian architecture and rejected the tower in favor of well-balanced vertical and horizontal lines. For this reason—and because the tower was also rejected on the basis of national considerations—the Gothic style never really became established, and there was an unbroken link between antiquity and the Renaissance.

In the Byzantine or Eastern Roman Empire, the tower never achieved any remarkable height in the central dome structure, with its bulbous roof. The creative wealth of popular art produced by the national variation of the Russian towers, however, can be demonstrated by the colorfulness of the few examples from Kiev and Moscow shown in this book. Here, too, the Gothic style did not exert a lasting influence on the development of different national forms.

With the logical development from the Romanesque to the Gothic style between 1000 and 1500, Central and Western Europe were the real centers for religious tower building. The Romanesque style valued buildings with many towers and did not achieve heights of any significance. From the abbey church Maria Laach, it can be seen that despite the organic inclusion of the towers in the basilica, they lead quite a separate existence with their clear-cut stereometric shape. Their ponderous walls are scarcely interspersed with ornamental elements, and the effect of the vertical lines is greatly vitiated by the horizontal bands. The towers have a defiant and fortresslike air, the expression of the Early Medieval Period, displaying its established position by a markedly militant spirit.

Often enough abbeys and churches were fortresses in the literal sense, especially along the route to the East taken by the colonizers. These ecclesiastical defensive structures, the most striking form of which was the fortified church (Albi) or the church citadels of Transylvania, naturally retained their massiveness, which gave them a Romanesque appearance even during the

Gothic Period. Still, with the rise in economic and technical possibilities and with new social structures, the main trend was toward lightness and openness, especially in connection with urban development.

Heralded in the Late Romanesque Period with its richness of decoration (Mainz Cathedral), the liberating ideas of the French Gothic achieved open walls and dizzy heights by using flying buttress systems, pointed arches, canopies and finials. Although the number of towers was reduced to two, or even one, their height now surpassed everything previously built by human hand (Beauvais, 502 feet high, collapsed 1573). At 466 feet, the tower of Strasbourg Minster remained the highest tower of the Middle Ages still in existence until the towers of Cologne Cathedral (512 feet) and Ulm Cathedral (528 feet), were completed in the 19th century on the basis of the old plans.

This shows that though the will was strong, it was often limited by what was actually possible. The filigreelike towers with their wealth of ornamentation and figures took an endless time to complete. Generation after generation of masons, organized in artisans' associations, handed down their secrets on the same project, created for the greater glory of God. The towers were open to the wind and rain and delicacy of detail was maintained even in places which were no longer visible to the eye. An impressive idea of the artistic and technical mastery of Gothic architecture is conveyed by the spire of Freiburg Cathe-

p. 50

dral, which is completely decorated with tracery.

On the southern edge of Europe, in the regions of Spain and the Balkans previously ruled by the Moors and the Turks, isolated examples of yet another type of religious tower are to be found, the minaret. It was usually separate from the main structure of the mosque and was built in many different forms, the slim type (Pécs, Constanţa) being preferred. From the upper platform, the muezzin summoned the followers of Allah to prayer from all sides. The specific functional purpose of this tower, combined with the inclination of Islamic architecture to decorate the interior more richly than the exterior, never allowed the Islamic minaret to achieve the importance of the medieval church tower.

In Moorish Spain, however, in the confrontation with Christendom, it would appear that the tower played a more significant role. After the recapture of Seville, the Giralda bell tower of the cathedral was increased to a height of 312 feet. It still has the massive substructure of a richly ornamented minaret. Next to it there is the splendid Torre del Oro, "the golden tower," which served for defense. Testimony to the bitterness of this struggle is still provided by the extensive fortifications of the Alhambra, the "red castle" of Granada, which, as the last bulwark, fell in 1492. However, the Spanish also attached great importance to the tower as a means of repulsing attacks. A glance at the Alcázar of Segovia, built by Alphonso VI in the 11th century, shows

that the steeply rising rock, with the walls surmounting it, was increased still further in height by towers.

The almost unbroken links between religious buildings and fortifications continued up to the close of the Middle Ages. Dogmatic religious ideas, symbolized by the self-sufficiency of the tower, were the necessary expression of this time of mighty social upheavals which, in turn, led to the fortified tower and gate. The castle, which is found in all nations from their very beginnings, became an eminently important task of construction for European communities in the Middle Ages. The knight's castle was the basis of local feudal power. For the serfs it was an instrument of oppression, but it was also a refuge and place of retreat during the numerous feuds between the knights, and in the knights' struggles against their overlords and against the towns, which were increasingly demanding independence.

The primary function, defense, always dictated a tower which made little claim to exceptional artistic merit, was not very high, but was of massive construction, thus forming part of an organic complex with the walls, living quarters, and other buildings. The gateway, which was extensively fortified, was likewise not decorated to any significant extent.

Of the exceptional range of forms in Europe, which varied greatly from one country to another, the Rocca Montale of San Marino may be regarded as a typical basic form. The rocky hill is crowned with walls and interspersed with towers, according to the

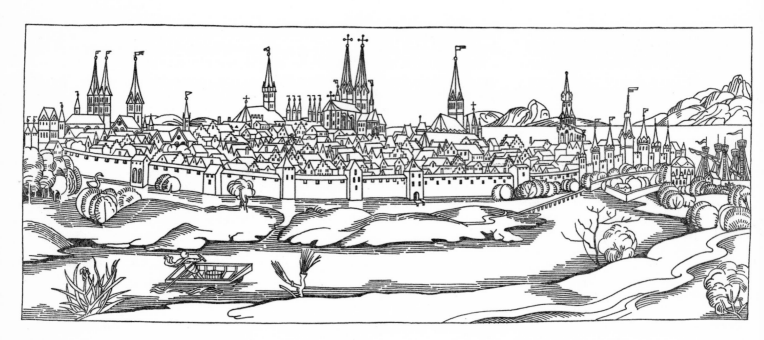

View of Lübeck. Drawing after a woodcut from Schedel's "Weltchronik"

nature of the terrain. As a symbol of defiance, the highest point was formed by a particularly stout tower, this being the lookout and the last place of retreat. Often this was the keep, with living quarters in its upper stories and standing apart from the other buildings so that it could be more easily defended, as illustrated here by the castle of Münzenberg. In France this type of residential tower, known as a "donjon," was even more marked. In England and Sicily, all functions were combined in a single mighty structure in the form of the towered castle (Termoli).

Most castles, built by the compulsory labor of the peasants, stood in majestic isolation with the villages spread out at their foot. Others, in their early stages, were protective centers of crystallization for the developing towns. Subsequently, with the growing economic power of the towns and their demand for self-government, the castles lost this function. Wherever these castles were not razed to the ground they stand as a sign of the times when the towns first started to emerge. The picturesque castle of the Counts of Nuremberg, the massive, water-encircled stronghold of the Counts of Flanders in Ghent, or the extensive brick kremlins—such as that of the Russian tsar built in Moscow in 1487—are evidence of the national diversity at the same stages of development in Europe.

A detailed explanation for the characteristic multitude of towers in the medieval town is hardly necessary. After a hesitant beginning in the 10th century, when use was still made of ancient ruins or of old earthen ramparts with wooden palisades, a continuous system of stone fortifications—with walls, towers, and gates—emerged in Central Europe in the course of the 12th century. This was necessary since the town privileges had to be wrested from the feudal lords and subsequently defended against them, and it was necessary to ensure that the various towns could compete successfully with other communities. Indeed, there were many reasons for the constant development of the system of defense.

If the profusion of church spires is added to this and, in the latter part of this period, the increasing numbers of communal towers (town hall towers, clock towers, water towers, etc.), it can well be imagined how the towers dominated the towns' relatively restricted areas and characterized the specific silhouette of every town. Early topographical works, such as Schedel's *Weltchronik* of 1493 and Merian's 30-volume *Topografie*, published between 1642 and 1688, made use of these "visiting cards." They also convey an idea of how many of the original towers of European towns have disappeared; only very few cities, such as Prague or Moscow, still give an approximate impression of the former profusion.

Most of the systems of fortifications were demolished in the 19th century because they hindered the expansion of the big cities and had long since lost their original purpose. A number of small towns in Europe still possess impressive walls. Their towers had a platform at the top with projecting battlements and often machicolations and arrow slits on the field side, so that every attack at the base of the walls could be effectively opposed by arrows fired from long bows or crossbows or, from the 14th century on, by guns.

The ever greater range of these weapons necessitated an increase in the spacing and thickness of the towers in the walls. The wall encircling Avila, built on ancient foundations in the 11th century, is 1.5 miles in length and has 86 closely spaced towers. The city wall of Avignon, on the other hand, just over three miles long and built 300 years later, has only 39 towers. For some time still, efforts were made to counteract the increase in firepower by building fortifications with thicker walls, broader moats, outworks, buttresses, and arches, plus double or triple rings of defense. But it was the cannon that ultimately won this contest in the 16th century. For another three centuries, low and extensive defense systems with star-shaped bastions were all that could be set against it, until eventually even these represented no obstacle to the latest instruments of warfare.

The gateway played a special role in the construction of medieval fortifications. It was the most vulnerable point but at the same time the most stately, symbolizing the power and the wealth of the city to the approaching stranger. It is consequently not surprising that 70 of the major 300 towns of Germany included a town gate in their coat of arms. The individuality and artistic quality of their design was the salvation of many gateways, mostly dating from the Gothic Period, when in later times town walls were pulled down; large numbers of gateways still exist today.

Their basic principle, which was already evolved in antiquity (Ishtar Gate, Porta Augusta), consisted of two towers joined by the arch of the gateway, this satisfying military requirements and representing a pleasing aesthetic image at the same time. The frequently protruding towers on each side of the gate enclosed the lower part of the arch so that the upper part represented an ideal surface for decorative or symbolic ornamentation. Horizontal artic-

Old coat of arms of Freiberg in Saxony

ulation and strict symmetry were the essential features of the design, despite the diversity of the national variations, whose wealth of ornamentation increased considerably at the end of the Middle Ages. Yet even the Holsten Gate at Lübeck, where the tendency was reversed, can convey the proud self-assurance of a free and mighty Hanseatic town solely by reason of its monumental dimensions.

Besides the double-towered gateway, there was also a single gate-tower in which the gateway was incorporated in the square substructure of the tower. With the invention of firearms, new designs were evolved, with the basic layout being a double set of gates and the barbican. The first of these designs consisted of an outer gateway which was linked by walls with the higher inner gateway. In the event of an enemy forcing an entry, he could be compelled to fight on three sides simultaneously within the narrow confines of the space between the two gateways. The Treptow Gate in Neubrandenburg is impressive evidence of the fact that these gates, too, were used as instruments of municipal dignity, despite their military character. With its contrasting and richly ornamented decoration, this gate is an outstanding example of the style typical of the brick architecture of the North. Finally, the barbicans were usually semicircular, towerlike structures located outside the moat; their task was to absorb the initial impetus of the attack on the gateway. Where bridges had to be protected, bridge towers were built, usually at the ends. Those of the Charles Bridge in Prague are probably the finest examples.

Numerous though they were in the Middle Ages, these secular towers and gateways were very seldom able to compete with ecclesiastical structures as far as architectural lavishness was concerned. Italy would appear to be the only exception. For reasons already referred to, the Italian church tower never achieved great significance. The worldly spirit of the emerging Renaissance and the desire for display of the rich city-states and the nobility resulted in the towers of the town halls and the family towers being built to tremendous heights. The slim towers, crowned by belfries, of the Palazzo Vecchio in Florence and the Torre del Mangia of the town hall in Siena are 315 and 325 feet high, respectively. Testimony to a victorious civic pride, the towers were valiant in appearance but without any real military function. Even the family towers of Umbrian and Tuscan

Battle scene from Herrad von Landsperg's "Hortus deliciarum"

towns such as San Gimignano or Bologna were symbols of aristocratic power rather than works of defense.

In the other parts of Europe, the tower was slow to become established in secular architecture with the exception of fortifications. The town hall, the center of bourgeois power, was the place where the tower could most often be found, but other communal buildings, such as those of the trades or guilds, also made use of this ancient symbol of display. Particularly elaborate and lofty were the belfries in Flanders, demonstrating the commercial prosperity of this country. As a rule, these secular structures served as bell or clock towers. Indeed, though it had been customary since the 13th century for the time of day to be indicated on the church tower, the wealth and artistic significance of municipal clock towers in the early years of the Renaissance—especially in Italy—are evidence of the worldliness of the civic spirit. Apart from its new technical achievements, the clock tower of the Old Town Hall in Prague is an attractive example of the inventive spirit and more penetrating insight of the new age.

For various reasons, the tower was not to enjoy so outstanding a position in the Renaissance as hitherto. Thus, developments in the art of war—the replacement of the hand-to-hand combat of armies of armored knights by the long-range actions of mercenary troops—meant that there was no longer any purpose in having castles and town fortifications. Both of these (the castle first, the town fortifications later) had to yield to the rising absolutist power of the reigning monarch. The king now resided in a castle which had lost nearly all of its defensive character, including the role of the wall and tower.

An interesting transitional form led to the magnificent towerless structures of the Baroque Period, with their splendid entrance halls. This form is represented by the staircase towers of Renaissance castles in France and Germany, which incorporate features from both epochs (the Château at Blois, Hartenfels Palace at Torgau). In the spiral Gothic manner, the staircase soars upward in the tower set against the facade. Yet this lavishly ornamented tower is open to the skies like a scaffold, does not exceed the roof of the main structure in height, and matches the horizontal lines of the facade in its articulation. This is a sign of an additional and generally valid reason for reducing the height of towers.

The Renaissance, with its respect for the classical emphasis on balance clearly preferred to make buildings longer rather than higher, or attempted to achieve a balance between the two dimensions. Renaissance architects did not favor Gothic verticalism. But the wealth of structural memories in the stylistic forms of the Renaissance and the subsequent Baroque Period proves that the legacy of the Gothic Period in architecture was never completely renounced north of the Alps.

Apart from this, towers with a functional purpose, such as bell, clock, fire, water, and harbor towers remained topical, of course.

The few examples here from the 16th to the 18th centuries illustrate the peculiar contradiction in tower construction of this period. As instanced by the Town Hall of Poznan, the harbor towers at Hoorn and Amsterdam, or the Exchange at Copenhagen, the upward rise of the tower was braked, as it were, by the stepped sections and a marked horizontality. There is no attempt to make the tower attain lofty heights, separating it from the structure as a whole. The mighty towers have become "towerlets," light and attractive with their curved helms and airy lanterns.

On the other hand, church architecture, which had receded far into the background during the Renaissance, came to the fore again in the course of the Counter-Reformation. It put new life into the Gothic tradition, especially in Southern Germany, and produced imposing single and twin towers. The 283-foot-high tower of the Catholic Court Church in Dresden, built by Chiaveri and his successors between 1739 and 1755, is an impressive example of this native tradition with its slim, perforated silhouette.

To an even greater extent than the tower, the gateway experienced a major change in design and, increasingly, in function as well. The thousand-year unity of tower and gateway disintegrated. The model of the triumphal arch of antiquity was revived once more and took the place of the fortified gateway. Where the gateway continued to be used in fortifications, a broad layout was employed, low and heavy like the bastions and with extensive bossage-work. Yet despite this adaptation to advances in the techniques of warfare, it became ever more obsolete, at least in its architectural significance.

The civic and, especially in the age of feudalism, princely desire to display wealth and position led to a revival of the triumphal arch. From the Baroque Period up into the age of Classicism, the triumphal arch continued to exist as the architectonic symbol of the monarchist claim to power. Sometimes it stood in an isolated position, other times it formed part of great squares, as at the Praça do Commercio in Lisbon or Palais Square in Leningrad. It is interesting to note that, despite the declared opposition of Classicism to Baroque style, there was no appreciable change in its design of the arch and attic. There is certainly a huge social epoch between the triumphal arch at Montpellier, erected in honor of Louis XIV in 1691, and the Arc de Triomphe of Napoleon in Paris, finally completed in 1836, but they are linked by the same spirit of autocracy.

The established layout of the triumphal arch, the loss of its function as a defensive structure and, associated with this, the reduction of the gateway to a wrought-iron portal in front of castles and gardens,

have led to only a few isolated examples of original work being produced. In widely varying ways, there is still a trace of the gateway-tower in the Crown Gate of the Zwinger in Dresden (1711–1722) and the Admiralty Gate in Leningrad (1806–1822). As light and graceful as a pavilion, the Crown Gate forms a part of an ornate Baroque complex, while the classic Admiralty Gate, heavy and massive, is like a church tower, symbolizing Russia's position as a new sea power. In contrast, the Brandenburg Gate (1788–1791) in Berlin or the Propylaea (1848–1862) at Munich combine, in a free interpretation, the classical model of the Propylaea at Athens with the idea of the triumphal arch.

Many of these ostentatious gates were built for a variety of reasons, even as recently as this century, but in most cases they are of little artistic merit. Unlike their role in the past, however, they were now symbols of official dignity with a collective basis, as shown by the history of exhibition architecture from the World Expositions in Paris to the Agricultural Exhibition in Moscow. The significance of the gate as such has disappeared. More practical considerations have prevailed. Wherever civic buildings justify the accentuation of the reception zone, as at railway stations, airports, seaports, government and communal buildings, sports stadiums, and so on, the expression of dignity is conveyed by the architecture as a whole, without special emphasis on the entrance. It is

occasionally the case, as illustrated by the entrance to the Technical Fair at Leipzig, that a symbolic design is employed, but this can scarcely be regarded as a gate.

The tower, on the other hand, experienced a new heyday with the 19th century. On the basis of the emergent capitalist industry, towers not only remained manifestations of power (parliament, town hall). They also performed a series of new and practical functions in industry, trade and communications, and science (water, drilling, cooling, gas and winding towers; lighthouses, bridge, observation, and exhibition towers; meteorological stations and observatories). Furthermore, the older functions of towers remained, and clock and bell towers in particular (as well as church towers) continued to be built.

A forest of towers arose but, unfortunately, quantity was not matched by originality. Without regard to the purpose of the particular tower, designs were based on models from the whole of history, from the Romanesque and Gothic periods, from Islamic architecture, from the Renaissance and Classicism. Even hybrids of the different styles were built. Despite this eclecticism, it has to be admitted that many of these structures achieved an impressive aesthetic effect. Nor must it be forgotten that the diversity of new tasks, which have not increased to any extent in the present century, could scarcely have been handled in the initial stages except by recourse to the stylistic features of the past.

Even civil engineering, which emerged under totally new conditions, paid tribute to the slogan "architecture means ornamentation." The imposing Eiffel Tower of the 1889 Paris International Exposition, 984 feet high and assembled from 12,000 component parts, is a combination of triumphal arch and obelisk. The truth of the dictum about unity of function, technology, and material in architecture was not yet accepted. Nor was the bourgeoisie, now that it had come to power and wealth, ready to cast off the bejeweled royal mantle of the past.

At the end of the 19th century, however, democratic and liberal forces of reform moved toward new stylistic principles which form the basis of present-day ideas. All the towers from this new period shown in this book, such as those of the city halls of Copenhagen and Stockholm, the "Hochzeitsturm" (Wedding Tower) by Olbrich in Darmstadt, or Bonatz's Railway Station Tower in Stuttgart, have one thing in common: they stress the domination of height by simple, unadorned structures. Like the Italian Family Towers of the Middle Ages, they make their impact solely through the impression of strength that they convey.

Yet the age of the stonemason and medieval reminiscences is past. The shapes of towers were revolutionized by new materials—steel, concrete, reinforced and prestressed concrete—new designs and constructional techniques, a new understanding of statics and aerodynamics. Tasks associated with radio, radar, and television, and the mighty increase in social potential, also played a key part. Thus it was possible for Mendelsohn, under the influence of Expressionism, to build the dynamic Einstein Tower at Potsdam in 1920–21. Thanks to the versatility of reinforced concrete, he was able to model it on the turret of a warship.

With this revolution, a shape of tower evolved which is no longer based on any particular layout. Towers can now be built which practically reverse the aesthetic principles that once applied to every tower; namely that the diameter had to decrease with the height, or at least that the same dimensions and symmetry had to be maintained. The impression of gravity-defying elegance can today be achieved, as instanced by the Water Tower at Lahti in Finland. This tower, erected in 1960, is over 130 feet in height. Its daring lines are an outstanding example of new concepts of beauty in tower design, the development of which is being furthered to a decisive extent by industrial methods of construction.

A final look at contemporary tower design in Europe seems to indicate that the creative fantasy of architects is allowed a completely free rein. Nevertheless, there is a strict discipline of rationalism beneath the surface. As diverse as the towers may appear to be, their essential stylistic features point to a specific period. They consistently stress the basic purpose-related form, a clarity of outline, and the intrinsic aesthetic charm of materials, structures, and colors. Often use is made of light, as well, and of vibrant proportions.

Nowadays, towers are mostly built for a specific purpose and only in church architecture or memorial structures do they seem to incorporate abstract concept (as instanced by the Bell Tower at the former concentration camp of Buchenwald). But the extension of function does in no way restrict the power of abstract expression. The historical review here has shown that even the tower erected for practical considerations can be, to a greater or lesser extent, the aesthetically designed instrument of specific social objectives.

Admittedly, many types need time to mature and to develop power of expression before attention is attracted to their architectonic qualities. The most revealing example of this is the rapid development of the most significant type of modern tower, the television tower, since the Second World War. With the triumphal advance of television, this type of tower has not only broken all altitude records within a decade (Berlin, 1,198 feet; Moscow, 1,763 feet) but, after a hesitant start, soon achieved an elegant and characteristic form. In many cities of Europe, such as Stuttgart, London, Berlin, and Moscow, its unmistakable shape is a feature of the city silhouette and its surroundings, testimony to the fact that even in the age of technological revolution there has been no decline in artistic creativeness.

INDEX OF PLACE NAMES

SOURCES OF ILLUSTRATIONS

Plates

MYCENAE, LION GATE

The Lion Gate of the fortress at Mycenae, on the edge of the rugged district of Argolis in Peloponnesus, is the earliest ornamented fortress gateway in Europe. It was built by the warlike Achaeans in the 14th century B.C. According to the *Iliad*, Homer's illustrious epic poem, it was from here that Agamemnon went to war against the Trojans. The colossal blocks of stone in what is left of the wall and the gateway—the lintel block over the gateway is $16^1/_2$ feet long and over eight feet thick—are the expression of the early Greeks' primitive urge to achieve monumentality. Legend says that these walls were built by the Cyclops.

On the 10-foot-high triangular relieving stone above the lintel block, two lions are carved, facing each other on either side of a column. These symbols of majesty were intended as a warning to potential enemies and originated in the Middle East. An impression of menacing power is conveyed here. Only after the occupation by the Dorians, who overran this aristocratic civilization of Mycenae in the 12th century B.C., were the foundations laid for the golden age of ancient Greece.

ATHENS, PROPYLAEA OF THE ACROPOLIS

The Propylaea of the Acropolis was built of Pentelic marble by Mnesicles in only six years, between 437 and 432 B.C. During this time the city-state of Athens was at the peak of its power. The speed with which it was built indicates that a propylaea such as this (literally "the square before the gate") was often a part of the monumental structure at the entrance to temple precincts, stadiums, or palaces. The propylaea of Mnesicles is one of the most beautiful, and is still impressive today, even as a ruin.

25

The chief reason for this dignified and well-balanced complex, extending from the foot of the hill to the platform at the top, was the procession during the chief festival of the Athenians, which climbed the steps to the Parthenon once every year. The architecture plays a noteworthy role in setting the atmosphere for this event of the Panathenaea. Through a massive, pylonlike gateway, the Greeks ascended a flight of steps on either side of a ramp for wheeled vehicles and sacrificial animals. The solemn Doric front of the upper part of the building formed, with the smaller wing structures extending forward on either side, a kind of ceremonial courtyard.

The illustration here is of the east facade. The exit toward the Parthenon is lined by slim Ionian columns. This unity of the different moods, ranging from majestic solemnity to festive relaxation, the wonderful harmony of all the parts in which the stimulating effect of the terrain is incorporated, is an architectural masterpiece which could only have evolved on the soil of early Greek democracy, with its emphasis on human dignity. Works of later ages based on this Classical Period, such as the Propylaea at Munich (1848–1862), could never be more than a reflection of the original achievement.

PERUGIA, PORTA AUGUSTA

The Porta Augusta at Perugia, erected in about 100 B.C., not only gives an indication of the different outlook of the Romans as compared with the Greeks—it is austere, functional, and at the same time has a greater element of display—but also conveys an idea of its Etruscan roots. The development of an extremely well-fortified type of gateway, with bastions extended far in front, aptly symbolizes the exceptionally turbulent course of Etruscan-Roman history. At precisely the time that the gate was built, a rebellion erupted when

Sardinia, Nuraghe

the Romans refused the right of citizenship to their Italic allies. Of significance for the future was the employment of the arch. Although it had already been known to the Babylonians, it had not been adopted by the Greeks. With this, the Romans created the prototype for the Middle Ages in Europe.

SARDINIA, NURAGHE
This type of tower, of which large numbers still exist on Sardinia and Corsica and in Southern Italy, dates back to the dawn of history. In Sardinia alone, there are still more than 7,000 of these simple beehive-shaped towers, built from rough stones without the use of mortar. On this island which was often under attack and which offered no way of escape, the nuraghi were the last refuge of the tribes. Because the entrance was high up and allowed only one man to pass at a time, it was easily defended. A spiral staircase let into the wall, provided access to the upper story, where there was space enough for up to 100 people and which also served as living quarters. On the lower level were the ancestral graves, evidence of the intimate and magical links between the living and the dead which were to be continued in the distinct ancestor-cult of the Romans.

ROME, TOMB OF CAECILIA METELLA
At the edge of the famous Via Appia near Rome lies the tomb, built *c.* 50 B.C., of Caecilia Metella, wife of Crassus the Younger, whose father was one of the Triumvirate. This edifice is 66 feet in diameter and almost as high. The upper part is encircled by the "bucranium" (the skulls of sacrificial bulls, often joined by garlands), a decorative frieze which was originally part of the altar. In the Middle Ages, when, on account of its size, this tomb was converted to a fortress by the aristocratic Caetani family, it was known locally as the 'Capo di Bove' (bull's head).

ATHENS, TOWER OF THE WINDS

In Athens, at the Roman Market, there is one of the few well-preserved towers of antiquity—the "Tower of the Winds," as it is known. Its name comes from the reliefs of the wind gods who decorate the upper part of the octagon below the roof. A weathercock, which no longer exists, was placed on the peak of the flat tent-roof; it pointed—according to the direction of the wind—to the respective god. There is also a sundial outside and a water clock inside. Greece had long been a Roman colony when this tower, which is only 39 feet high, was built *c.* 50 B.C. by a foreigner, the Syrian Andronicus of Kyrrhestis. This tower is of great interest from the viewpoint of social history.

ROME, TRIUMPHAL ARCH OF SEPTIMIUS SEVERUS

According to the inscription on the attic, this triumphal arch on the Forum Romanum was dedicated to the emperor Septimius Severus in A.D. 203 by the Senate and the People in commemoration of his victories over the Parthians. Arches such as this were built by the Empire from the second century B.C. onward in honor of its successful generals. The victor drove through the arch with his legions and the spoils of war, this representing a symbolic cleansing act. Originally, the arches were of simple construction, but the Arch of Septimius Severus is a typical instance of the love of magnificence and the dictatorial pretensions of the soldier-emperors. It was thanks to his legions that in Pannonia, Severus was able to defeat two rivals and become the emperor.

Because of the constant threat to the supreme power, it became increasingly important to demonstrate this supremacy at the Forum Romanum, that place were the greatness of the Roman Empire and its history were displayed in concentrated

form. The height of this triumphal arch (76 feet) and its exceptional ornateness show how Severus attempted to outclass his predecessors.

Even the sculptures have been used to proclaim his fame. The legionnaires literally support the columns of his power, which was exclusively of a military character. The subject peoples were represented above the side arches, and the figures of the goddesses of victory topped the principal arch. The arch was surmounted by a gigantic bronze group, consisting of the emperor and his sons, Geta and Caracalla, on a chariot drawn by six horses, but this has not been preserved.

ROME, ARCH OF CONSTANTINE

More than a century later, between A.D. 312 and 315, the emperor Constantine, after defeating his rival Maxentius, had the Senate build him a triple triumphal arch. This was done within a very short time. The disregard of the past during this stormy period of the Empire, with all its internal strife, is shown by the unscrupulous way in which Constantine plundered a whole series of older monuments in order to make his as magnificent as possible. (Statues along the attic and the central arch are from the time of Trajan; the attic reliefs are from the arch of Marcus Aurelius.) All that comes from Constantine's own era are the reliefs at the base depicting legionnaires and their captives, the victory figures and river gods in the spandrels, the narrow strips in relief above the side-arches, and the busts of Constantine and other emperors.

The coarseness evident in this work, and the piecemeal character of the triumphal arch as a whole, are an indication of a deterioration in creative power. That people in later times were also unscrupulous in the way they treated the legacy of the past is demonstrated by the fact that this arch was later incorporated in the medieval fortress of the Frangipani, from which it was not freed until 1804.

ROME, PORTA SAN PAOLO (PORTA OSTIENSIS)

The Porta Ostiensis, known as the Porta San Paolo since the Middle Ages, is one of the mightiest fortification structures of the end of the 3rd century. It was built to safeguard the metropolis of Rome. The increasing frequency of the raids by border peoples on the weakened Empire had obliged the emperor Aurelian to erect the massive Aurelian Wall (56 feet high, 13 feet thick), with 300 towers and 13 gates in the shortest time possible, between 271 and 280, using forced labor. Thus the city was able to hold out until the relief army came. The type of fortified gateway already developed in Perugia (Porta Augusta) is retained,

the protruding round towers being the only additional feature of the Porta San Paolo. In contrast to the triumphal arch, it has no ornamentation, and it kept its defensive function until the end of the Middle Ages.

Near the gate is the pyramid tomb of the tribune Gaius Cestius. This structure, which is over 120 feet high and was completed in 330 days nearly 2,000 years ago, was converted into a bastion in 1410 but was restored to its original appearance in 1660.

ISTANBUL, WALL OF THEODOSIUS

Constantinople, now known as Istanbul, became the capital of the Eastern Roman Empire in a time of decline from within and attack from without (the final division of the Roman Empire taking place in 395). In the decades when the Roman legions were still strong enough to defeat the foe far from the cities, no defensive works were needed. How necessary they subsequently became is proved by the unsuccessful storming of the walls of Constantinople by the Goths, victorious in the battle against the emperor Valens in 378. The emperors Theodosius I and Theodosius II consequently made it their business to put one of the mightiest walls of all around the capital, which was particularly

Istanbul, Wall of Theodosius
Ravenna, San Apollinare Nuovo

exposed to danger on the land side. This was done *c.* 400. The wall has three lines of defense, 96 towers, and 29 gates. Colored strips in the walls are the only decoration of this battlemented system of fortifications which withstood every attack for many centuries.

RAVENNA, SAN APOLLINARE NUOVO

Theodoric, the king of the Ostrogoths and at the same time the representative of the Byzantine emperor on Italian soil, resided in Ravenna for the 33 years of his reign (493–526). He erected a series of structures in which features of the Roman empires are blended with Germanic elements. His principal church, that of San Apollinare Nuovo, built about the year 500, is a brickwork basilica with a completely undecorated exterior but with a splendid mosaic interior.

The campanile is just as plain, the only articulation of this massive cylindrical structure being the zones of double and triple windows. The isolated position of the bell tower at the side of the basilica was the typical tower layout for Italian church architecture for another thousand years.

SALONIKA, TRIUMPHAL ARCH OF GALERIUS

In Salonika, there still stands the imposing central arch of a triumphal arch erected by Gaius Galerius about A.D. 300. He was one of the commanders appointed by Diocletian in A.D. 293 to rule the vast provinces of the Balkans and Greece. In a ruthless struggle with his rivals, he attained the rank of Augustus in 305. To build a monument to oneself was something which was taken for granted by that time. This arch of brick masonry is covered in relief figures depicting the deeds of this soldier-emperor. Under the influence of the East, the stylistic features have become harder and sharper, yet what is lost in organic vitality

s compensated by the emerging richness of form, the future characteristic of Byzantine art.

TRIER, PORTA NIGRA

In the provinces they conquered, the Romans built castles and fortified towns. In Trier, which was developed as an important base on the frontier along the Rhine to oppose the Germanic tribes, there still exists the massive Porta Nigra. It is the finest structure dating from the time of Cassianus Latinus Postumus, the ruler during the Roman-Gallic period of the Empire. This double-arched building, erected about A.D. 260, is more than a defensive structure. With its dimensions of 95 feet high, 118 feet long, and 52 and 72 feet deep, with its double gallery, with the elaborate facade decorated by columns, it is the magnificent symbol of imperial power. This structure, which is complete in itself, is like a castle with a gateway. In the 12th century it was turned into a church, but Napoleon had it restored to its original appearance so that the beauty of the ancient architecture could be fully appreciated.

PISA, CATHEDRAL AND CAMPANILE (LEANING TOWER OF PISA)

The most famous tower in the world, the out-of-line campanile of the cathedral at Pisa, is also one of the most beautiful examples of the Italian Romanesque period at its best. Its cylindrical core, which follows the Ravenna pattern, is enclosed by six gracious galleries of marble columns. A heavy belfry interspersed with colored elements crowns the top. It forms a harmonious group with the cathedral (1063–1183) and the baptistery (begun in 1152), which can be seen in the background. It owes its fame, however, not so much to its beauty but to its imperfection, which has remained uncorrected despite a dramatic history of construction.

In 1174, Master Bonanus of Pisa laid apparently adequate foundations for it in the marshy ground, driving tree-trunks in as piles and using a stone bed 62 feet deep. The tilt to the south was soon noticed and an attempt was made to compensate for this by steadily increasing the height of the south side, but Bonanus gave up after reaching the third gallery. Master Wilhelm of Innsbruck, however, took over in 1234 and, using the same principle of correction, continued until the last gallery was reached. The belfry was finally added by Thomas of Pisa in 1350. The tower, 179 feet in height, is slightly curved toward the north on account of the greater height of the south side. Since completion of the tower, the tilt has steadily increased. As far back as 1589, Galileo is believed to have used it in the elaboration of the laws of falling bodies. (Dropping a number of heavy stones from the top gallery enabled him to draw the conclusion that regardless of the weight of the stones, they constantly acquire more speed as they fall.)

At the present time, the tower is 14 feet off perpendicular at the top, the tilt increasing by about a millimeter every year. A number of proposals for saving the tower have been submitted in an international competition; if, these do not work, the collapse of the tower is only a question of time. Due to a similar tilt, the bell tower of Saragossa fell in 1887. Whether the usual technique, halting the movement of the foundations by the injection of cement, will effect a cure remains to be seen.

SIENA, CAMPANILE OF THE CATHEDRAL
High above the Tuscan town of Siena, situated on the top of a hill, there rises the cathedral with its slim, square-section campanile from the Gothic Period. Yet apart from the tiny towers at the corners there is nothing Gothic about it. Like all

campanili before, it soars upward without diminution, its straightness being lightened only by the arcade windows which become broader with every story. Its marked horizontal articulation is accentuated still further by the black and white stripes of the marble facing. The campanile is unusual in that it is included in the wall enclosing the cathedral.

LORSCH, MONASTERY GATEHOUSE

An outstanding illustration of the survival of Roman ideas in relation to gateways and triumphal arches during the Carolingian period is the gateway of the monastery at Lorsch in Hesse. Built about 800, the two-storied building with round staircase towers at either end has a flat-roofed open hall with three round arches. It is believed that the upper story was used as an imperial court of judgment before being consecrated as a chapel to St. Michael. The steep roof is a Gothic addition.

The lightness of the design and the magnificent architectural decoration—half-columns and pilasters supporting composite capitals, the frieze of the fascia and the mosaiclike red-and-white stone facing—show that the gatehouse was not a fortified structure but an architectural symbol of imperial power. The ancient layout of the triumphal arch lives on, but the ornamental surface decoration and the row of triangular gables have not come from antiquity. Two hundred years were still to pass before the Romanesque period, following the conscious but not fully successful attempt here to recall the past, was able to evolve its own interpretation of the Roman model.

LAACH, ABBEY CHURCH MARIA LAACH
The church of the Benedictine abbey Maria
Laach near Lake Laach in the Eifel district is one
of the finest churches of the Late Romanesque
Period in Germany. It was founded in 1093 by
Heinrich II, Count of the Palatinate. The west
choir was consecrated in 1156 and the towers were
completed *c.* 1200. About 20 years later, a three-
winged atrium, known as the "Paradise," was
added in the west. The silhouette of this mighty
building with its two choirs, seen here from the
northwest, is marked by six towers—two crossing towers, two round staircase towers in the west,
and two towers in the east.

This profusion of towers in German Romanesque
is quite different from that in Russian architecture
of the same period. In Germany, the towers are
strictly articulated in the compact Romanesque
ground plan, and rise up as clearly differentiated
parts of the structure. They are decorated with
restraint and carry simple tent or rhomboid roofs.
This emphasizes the towers as such, although each
of them is linked with the others in the overall
concept, the size and severity of which underline
the spirit of feudal and ecclesiastical power symbolized here. The fortresslike impression is no accident.

SPLIT, CAMPANILE OF THE CATHEDRAL

The free-standing campanile is also found outside Italy, in other countries of Southern Europe. A bell tower 200 feet high and richly articulated by column arcades was erected in the 13th century in Split, on the coast of Yugoslavia. Based on Italian models, it is located on the terrain of the gigantic palace of Diocletian, on the west side of the cathedral which was originally his cupola-covered mausoleum. In the foreground a row of columns, a peristyle from the period about A.D. 300, can still be seen. This picture, with witnesses of different epochs mingling together, impressively demonstrates the close links between Roman and Romanesque architecture.

KIEV, CATHEDRAL OF ST. SOPHIA

The cathedral of St. Sophia, principal church of the Grand Duchy of Russia, was built by Prince Yaroslav between 1017 and 1037. It is one of the finest examples of early Russian architecture, which reached its climax in the grand duchy of Vladimir-Suzdal. Grounded in the Greek Orthodox religion and in the Byzantine tradition, it represents a national variation which is exceptional for its use of decoration and towers. Admittedly, the towers are not of any great height. Their outstanding characteristic is their number, which corresponds to the profusion of small rooms, and their onion-shaped cupolas with their upswept crests. Up to the Renaissance and even into the Baroque Period, the gilded onion-shaped cupola was the most striking part of towers symbolizing homage to God.

MOSCOW, CATHEDRAL OF ST. BASIL THE BLESSED

On Red Square in Moscow, there is a jewel of Russian national architecture: the Cathedral of St. Basil the Blessed, formerly known as Pokrovsky Sobor. It was built between 1554 and 1560 during the reign of Ivan the Terrible by Barma and Postnik, in honor of Mary and eight saints. It is almost unmarked by Byzantine influence, and largely free of Western European Renaissance forms as well. Triumphant here is a vitality of decoration and color from popular art. The nine imaginatively designed small towers surrounding the large main tower seem almost haphazard in their arrangement, yet this is based on the principle of a symmetrical central composition. Each of the typical onion roofs, artistically constructed of wood, has a different decoration and different colors. This group of towers, probably the most picturesque in Europe, fully expresses the Russian national character in the epoch of the Renaissance.

MOSCOW, KREMLIN, "IVAN THE GREAT" BELL TOWER

With its height of almost 270 feet, the "Ivan the Great" bell tower is still the highest of all the buildings of the Kremlin in Moscow. Standing away from the main structure like a campanile, the tower soars upward in three stages, with successive reductions in diameter. Without doubt, the unusual position of the tower is to be attributed to the influence of the ideas of the Italian Renaissance, which is also evident in the architectural details. Yet the wealth of decorative elements and the onion cupola clearly mark this tower, begun in 1532 and completed in 1600 during the reign of Boris Godunov as a typical example of the Russian Renaissance. The contrast in color between the white structure of the tower and the golden cupola is a characteristic feature.

44

Moscow, Kremlin, "Ivan the Great" Bell Tower

45

MAINZ, CATHEDRAL

The cathedral at Mainz, with those at Worms and Speyer one of the three Imperial Cathedrals of the Rhineland, is a two-choir structure of powerful appearance. The illustration shows the west choir, built between 1200 and 1239, with its three towers—the slim pair of choir towers and the great crossing tower. They constitute one of the finest groups of the Late Romanesque Period, and their wealth of forms, giving a more open treatment of the wall areas, hint at the approach of the Gothic Period. Indeed, the increase in the height of the crossing tower carried out in the 15th century scarcely stands out from the Late Romanesque part of the structure. Even the Baroque roofs of the towers, added by Franz Ignaz Michael Neumann in 1774 after the fire of 1767, fit in well with the wealth of decoration. This was an unusually early instance of respect and consideration for an existing structure.

ALBI, CATHEDRAL

In the year 1282, a few decades after the Albigensian Crusades, the bloody heretical uprisings directed against the Church, the cathedral of St. Cécile was built like a defiant fortress in the town of Albi, in the South of France. The massiveness of this archiepiscopal fortified church recalls the Romanesque Period. Originally, battlements and machicolations even heightened this impression of a fortress. Flanked by two staircase towers, the 259-foot-high main tower rises up in the west like a *donjon*. Its lighter upper story was added later, in the 15th century. The use of brick as a building material is unusual for France.

Reims, Cathedral

Laon, Cathedral

REIMS, CATHEDRAL

The coronation church of the kings of France, the cathedral of Reims is one of the greatest creations of the classic Gothic Period of the 13th century. This unusual view of the west towers, which were not completed until the 15th century, shows the advance of the urge toward verticality. There is a profusion of soaring decorative forms, each rising from another as it were, of half-columns, profiles, pointed arches, false gables, and finials. Horizontal lines are obscured everywhere. From the foot of the structure, the naked eye can no longer appreciate in full the extravagance of the meticulous work of the stonemasons. But this work was for the glory of God, who was above human standards of aesthetics.

LAON, CATHEDRAL

The towers of the cathedral, built at the end of the 12th and the beginning of the 13th centuries, soar high above the town of Laon in the North of France. Still Romanesque in the square-built compactness of their basic shapes and in their details, the towers nevertheless point to the Gothic Period in the treatment of the walls and in the airy corner-tabernacles, which grow slimmer as they rise upward. This bold approach was a pioneering contribution to the development of the Gothic open-work tower, the other feature of which—the verticality of the supporting columns—had already been anticipated in the French Early Gothic Period.

The extent of the symbolic content in the towers is demonstrated not only by the curiosity of the cattle visible in the top tabernacles of the west towers, which are a reference to a legend, but also by the association with the portal structure, recalling a triumphal arch. Like majestic guardians, the towers mark the entrance to the "heavenly Jerusalem."

FREIBURG, CATHEDRAL

The west tower of the cathedral at Freiburg im Breisgau, with its height of more than 380 feet, again demonstrates the Gothic desire to reach out toward the sky, and the Gothic self-sufficient technical and artistic mastery. About 1275, instead of laying the foundations for the customary front with two towers, it was wisely decided to build only a single main tower, which was completed some 75 years later. The beauty of the spire, octagonal in form and consisting entirely of filigreelike tracery, is unmatched in Europe. Its unknown creator was called a "Mozart" of architecture (W. Pinder). The imagination and boldness which he applied to the tracery of the spire in particular prove that he must have been an exceptionally strong personality, who was able to express himself in full despite his subordinate position and the

limitations of the time. Despite the different scale of the buildings, the view of the narrow streets from the octagonal tower even today conveys an impression of what medieval towns must have looked like when seen from towers such as this.

ULM, CATHEDRAL

In gratitude and to celebrate their victory over the imperial knights in 1377, the citizens of Ulm decided to build the biggest and most beautiful church of Germany. Although the town had only 12,000 inhabitants at that time, it was rich enough to implement this ambitious plan. In 1392, Ulrich Ensinger, the most famous tower architect of the Middle Ages, took over and continued the project with full vigor. Due to the slow rate of construction, he was not able to bring it to a successful conclusion.

With space for 30,000 people, Ulm Cathedral has the largest interior of all churches, but the attempt to achieve a record height was not successful. The foundations were only nine feet deep, and this was not enough. In 1492, cracks appeared in the tower, which had reached the halfway mark under the supervision of Matthäus Böblinger. He received the blame for this and was dismissed. An attempt was made to give added support to the tower by inserting walls where possible, but in 1529, after the Reformation, the work in which five generations had participated was abandoned. It was not until 1890 that the tower was completed according to Böblinger's plans and reached the intended height of 528 feet. It is the highest church tower in the world.

STRASBOURG, MINSTER

With its height of 466 feet, the tower of Strasbourg Minster, one of the greatest structures of the Middle Ages, is the highest of this epoch still standing. Its construction illustrates, in a very in-

Pécs, Minaret

structive manner, the change that took place within the Gothic Period. The mighty west front with its filigreelike verticality which continued through five stages of construction, since 1276, is still based on the design of Erwin von Steinbach.

After the victory of the citizens of Strasbourg over their bishop, who did not want to continue the project, Ulrich Ensinger, the architect of Ulm Cathedral, was commissioned by the town authorities in 1399 to take over the work on the north tower, no resources being available for the south one. This Late Gothic master used the graceful, spiral corner staircases to lift the tower into the air, as it were. Finally, between 1419 and 1439, Johannes Hültz added the spire that crowns it. With its profusion of complicated decorative elements and its 52 stepped finials, it rises up like a tongue of flame.

Even in Master Erwin's time, Strasbourg Cathedral had the reputation of being one of the most beautiful of Europe. With their own specific achievements, Ensinger and Hültz, architects of equal stature, consolidated its fame and helped the cathedral builders of Strasbourg to win a dominating position in Europe. The 23-year-old Johann Wolfgang von Goethe, however, believed that Master Erwin alone was responsible for it. He wrote a hymn to the master and his work. *Wie oft bin ich zurückgekehrt, von allen Seiten, aus allen Entfernungen, in jedem Licht des Tages zu schauen seine Würde und Herrlichkeit.* ("How often I have returned from any direction, from any distance, in any light of day, to behold its dignity and glory.") Recent research has brought to light the forgotten names of the other architects.

SEVILLE, GIRALDA BELL TOWER AND TORRE DEL ORO
The most famous tower of Spain is the Giralda bell tower of Seville Cathedral. It has the typical

national features of Spanish architecture which, in the confrontation with the Moors, resulted from the fusion of Moorish characteristics with European developments in style. The fortified minaret of the former mosque, built between 1184 and 1194, with its network and indented ornamentation formed the massive lower part. After 1568, following an earthquake, Hernán Ruz added a magnificently decorated bell tower, thus extending the structure to a height of over 300 feet. The extravagance of the characteristic wealth of decoration is testimony to the despotic urge of the Catholic Church to display its power in the period following the "Reconquista," when it dominated the intellectual life of Spain.

In the foreground, to the left, is another example of this unusual architecture, the Torre del Oro or "Golden Tower." This tower was once part of the Arab Alcázar (castle) and was built as a fortified structure by the governor Sid Abul Ala about 1220. Its name comes from the golden faience glaze which formerly decorated it. The windows and the stepped upper section with the golden cupola are a Spanish addition of the 18th century.

PÉCS, MINARET

The Turks occupied Hungary for almost two centuries, and a typical example of Islamic architecture is this minaret built about 1600 in Pécs. Like a campanile, but not so high or elaborate in design, this slim structure is located next to the mosque in the customary manner. From the upper platform, reached by a narrow spiral staircase on the inside, it was not a bell but the muezzin who called the faithful to prayer. The shape of the minaret recalls that of a column, and in point of fact the assumption that it could be based on the triumphal column of antiquity is justified.

CONSTANȚA, MINARET

The Rumanian port of Constanța also possesses a minaret from the period of Turkish domination, this one resembling a 19th-century lighthouse. Narrow window-slits provide light for the spiral staircase inside, which leads up to the projecting platform at the top. The platform was fitted with a roof in more recent times.

GRANADA, TOWERS OF THE ALHAMBRA

The Moors, forced back to the southern tip of Spain, fought back stubbornly until their last bulwark, the Residence of Granada, fell in 1492. The gigantic area of the Alhambra (literally "Red Castle"), built on a rocky plateau, is magnificent evidence of their achievements. With its interior resembling a tale from *Thousand and One Nights* and an exterior of undecorated severity, the massive fortifications provide excellent testimony to the high level of this Arab civilization. The Moors utilized the heritage of antiquity at an earlier stage than medieval Europe.

SAN MARINO, ROCCA MONTALE

The mountain town of San Marino in the independent state of the same name (area: 64 square kilometers) in the Apennines is crowned by the Rocca Montale, situated like a fortress on the rocks of Monte Citano. The fortifications form a separate entity and are linked with the medieval town wall, seen at the left of the picture. The main tower with its battlements was increased in height during the 20th century, its original form being retained.

SEGOVIA, ALCÁZAR

Many fortifications in Spain still bear witness to the savage struggles during the bloody "Reconquista." One of the most impressive of these is the Alcázar of the kings of Castile in Segovia, which dates from the 11th century. The picture shows the narrow side of this many-towered castle on the rocky western spur. Like the Arabs, from whom the Spaniards borrowed many an idea, the builders exploited the features of the terrain, and the fortress presents a picturesque and romantic sight. At the time of its construction, however, it was a symbol of aggressive royal power.

NUREMBERG, SINWELL TOWER

The Sinwell Tower (Old German "sinwell" = round) survived the serious damage sustained in the Second World War by Nuremberg, which had possessed the strongest medieval fortifications of Germany. This tower was erected as the keep of the castle of the burgraves in the 13th century. When an out-and-out struggle developed in the 14th century over the question of municipal right, the citizens of Nuremberg built a high tower nexts to the castle in 1377. In this way, their aristocratic foe could be kept under constant observation. The mighty trading city was the victor in this trial of strength and purchased the castle from the Hohenzollerns.

The two-part roof was fitted to the gloomy Sinwell Tower in 1560, heralding the advancing spirit of the Renaissance, which, coming from Italy, entered Germany through Nuremberg.

Today, this picturesque corner of the castle, far above the bustle of the big city, is more a place for peace and quiet reflection than might be thought if one were to look back on its eventful and stormy past.

Münzenberg, Castle
Termoli, Citadel

MÜNZENBERG, CASTLE

Of the numerous castles of the German knights
which had a massive, free-standing tower—the
keep—as a last place of refuge, Münzenberg in
Hesse is an exception since it possesses two. The
picture shows the view from the platform of one
of them looking toward the other, a plain round
tower with the typical high entrance, accessible
only via a ladder and easily defended. On the
various levels inside towers such as these, there
was everything that the inhabitants needed. At
floor-level, there was the storeroom and often
enough the dungeon; on the level of the entrance,
the kitchen and sleeping quarters for the bonds-
men; above this, the heated room for the lord of
the castle and his family; and, on the upper platform, the wooden shelter of the tower lookout. He
could see far beyond the villages of the Wetterau
area across which the shadow of this castle once
lay and could detect the approach of an enemy in
good time. Now a ruin, Münzenberg is a much-
visited tourist attraction.

TERMOLI, CITADEL

High above the little episcopal town of Termoli
on the Adriatic coast of Italy, there rises this
massive 13th-century three-level citadel. This
tower castle with its symmetrical plan was, because
of its restricted area, easier to defend than an
extensive system of fortifications. It functioned as
a residence and trade center as well. Similar structures existed in other parts of Europe, for instance
on Sicily, in England and France with an altered
form of the donjon.

Ghent, Castle of the Counts of Flanders

Windsor, Castle Gateway

GHENT, CASTLE OF THE
COUNTS OF FLANDERS

In the East Flemish city of Ghent, a prosperous center of the wool and cloth trade in the Middle Ages, there lies the "Gravensteen," the most important moat-castle of Western Europe. Like many castles, it was initially a fortress for the defense of the town but later became the menacing symbol of feudal power. It was constantly extended until the 14th century. The massive main building dates from about 1180. Twenty-nine small, semicircular towers, organically linked with the surrounding wall by buttresses, increase the defensive capability of the castle.

WINDSOR, CASTLE GATEWAY

In the county of Berkshire, on the banks of the Thames, there lies the "Royal Borough" of Windsor, with the ancient residence of the kings of England, Windsor Castle. Started by William the Conqueror and altered frequently up into the 19th century, it is certainly a charming sight now. The fine gateway, which dates from the late Middle Ages and is flanked by two polygonal towers, is crowned by battlements in the typical English manner.

FROMBORK, COPERNICUS TOWER

The plainly built Copernicus Tower in the late medieval town wall of the little Polish port of Frombork is of historical rather than architectural interest. It was here that one of the intellectual giants of the Renaissance, Nicholas Copernicus, carried out his astronomical observations for three decades in the years following 1512. The wooden brattices, which have been restored, convey a good idea of the usual layout of the interior-wall defensive system of the fortifications at that time.

MILAN, CASTELLO SFORZESCO

In 1368, the aristocratic Visconti family built a citadel in Milan to defend its interests. This was stormed by the people in 1447 and razed to the ground. Three years later, Duke Francesco Sforza had a new castle built on the same site, having a symmetrical front, flanked by two massive towers at the corners. The meticulous treatment of the pillow ashlar of the left tower, illustrated here, is an expression of the growing demand for decoration in the early years of the Renaissance.

MOSCOW, KREMLIN WITH SPASSKY TOWER

The heart and the oldest area of Moscow is the Kremlin, situated on a hill on the banks of the Moscow River. It is enclosed by a brick wall, $1^{1}/_{4}$ miles long, 90 feet high, and with 18 towers, dating from the second half of the 15th century. As the seat of the tsars, many churches and palaces were added in the course of the following centuries so that it became the symbol of Moscow and the whole of Russia. Its architecture determined the further development of Russian national architecture.

Even today, the Kremlin symbolizes the Soviet Union. The government, whose seat it has been since 1918, has consequently taken good care of the Kremlin—which is not only the biggest fortress complex of Europe but also one of the finest and most representative—and has maintained it in its original historical form. The illustration shows the view from the vestibule of the Church of St. Basil the Blessed looking toward the Spassky Tower. With a height of 236 feet, it is the highest tower in the wall enclosing the Kremlin. It was built like a stronghold by the Italian Mario Ruffo in 1491, and the Englishman Halloway, in 1625, added the neo-Gothic upper part and a big clock. The clock was rebuilt in 1851 and the famous bells renovated, whose chimes have been broadcast all over the world by Moscow Radio.

The characteristic silhouette of this fine tower and the charm of its formal decoration and colors have made it a symbol of Moscow. At night, the red star of the Soviet Union on top of the tower can be seen far and wide.

RILA MONASTERY, KRELYO TOWER

In the middle of the wooded Rila mountain range in Western Bulgaria lies Rila monastery, a gem of medieval Bulgarian architecture. For the forti-

fication of the monastery, which was often in danger, Prince Krelyo had the watch tower, which bears his name, built in 1335. Over 75 feet in height, its supporting pillars form part of an arcade. There is a chapel and living accommodation on the upper floor, and the platform at the top is lined with battlements. A bright and airy two-level loggia in cheery Renaissance style has been built onto the somber old tower.

ROTHENBURG, TOWN WALL
High above the Tauber Valley is Rothenburg, probably the best-preserved medieval town of the Federal Republic of Germany. The town wall dates from the 14th and 15th centuries, and with its individually named towers, set at varying distances from each other, conveys a lively impression of the technique of defense. A covered way, carried on pillars and cornels, runs around the entire wall on a level with the battlements. Passing through the towers, it ensured that communication could be maintained. Being well-protected, the citizens of the town, with cross-bow and gun, could effectively repulse any attack which crossed the first lines of defense.

AVILA, TOWN WALL
The most impressive example of old Spanish town fortifications is offered by Avila which, even today, is not much bigger than it was in the past. Situated on a rocky crag, the wall was built under the constant threat of attack during the momentous wars of the "Reconquista" in the surprisingly short time of nine years (1090–1099). The wall is 1½ miles in circumference, is built of granite blocks, and has 86 towers and nine gates. It must be mentioned, however, that use was made of what was left of ancient fortifications dating from the Roman period when the town was known as Abyla.

CARCASSONNE, CASTLE AND CITÉ

The town of Carcassonne in the South of France is still enclosed by one of the most impressive systems of fortifications in Europe. The Visigoths erected fortifications as far back as the 5th century on the strategically well-placed terrain of the cité, the higher part of the town. These fortifications were completely rebuilt between 1248 and 1285, giving the cité the character of a mighty fortress.

The cité is surrounded by a double town wall in which there are 54 towers. The profusion of the picturesque, interlinking parts of the various kinds of towers—the clear, cubic lines of which are typical for Southern Europe—was due to technical considerations of defense. If the enemy succeeded in forcing an entry, he could be sealed off in a restricted space.

AVIGNON, TOWN WALL WITH TOWER

In the 14th century, the town of Avignon on the banks of the Rhône was the residence of the banished popes, who erected a fortresslike palace on the 200-foot-high chalk cliff. Between 1350 and 1368, they built a thick wall more than three miles long around the town itself, the wall having eight gates and 39 towers. The illustration of a part of the wall shows the enormous scale of this system of fortifications, the height of which was even more impressive in the past, when there was still a moat here. A striking impression is conveyed by the system's symmetry, the fine craftsmanship of the stonemasons, and the cornices, with their volute decoration, projecting far out. As compared with more sober fortifications, such as those of Rothenburg, this is an example of an almost majestic type of architecture.

TOLEDO, PUERTA DEL SOL

After recovering Toledo from the Moors in 1085 the Spaniards, utilizing the existing defenses,

erected a magnificent Sun Gate, the Puerta del Sol. The unusual location of the gate in a corner of the wall called for a bastion of compact design so that the towers do not stand out; the left one is rounded off. In contrast to the plain town wall, however, the gateway is decorated in an imposing manner. Romanesque elements (such as the frieze of crossed arches) are blended with Moorish features (lancet arches and horseshoe arch gateway) to form the specifically national Mozarabic style, as it is known. Apart from this, the reliefs over the gateway proclaim the absolute supremacy of the militant Spanish Church.

VALENCIA, SERRANOS TOWERS

The Torres Serranos at the North Gate of the Mediterranean town of Valencia, which had already been fortified by the Romans, are a fine example of Gothic architecture. In fact, this double-towered gate was erected on Roman foundations in the 14th century. The polygonal towers with the gallery linking them are open on the side facing the town. The balanced proportions of this structure give an impression of strictness and strength, while there is a reserved delicacy in the decoration of the face in Mudéjar style, an amalgam of Gothic and Moorish forms.

BURGOS, ARCH OF SANTA MARIA

In comparison with the severe gateway in Valencia, the broad Arch of Santa Maria in Burgos, with the low, semicircular towers flanking it, is more like a splendid ornamental wall. It must be said, however, that the rich decoration in relief—figures of illustrious Spaniards (Ruy Diaz de Vivar, El Cid; Charles V; and others), the Guardian Angel above, the Madonna in her baldachin—was not part of the original design when the gateway was built between 1536 and 1552. They were added only in the 17th century, when the gateway itself

Basle, Spalen Gate

was of little value for defense. Nevertheless, the numerous slits for firearms, especially in the upper zone crowned by the four towers known as the Cubos, are an indication of its original function.

BASLE, SPALEN GATE
The Spalen Gate, built about 1400, is probably the finest medieval gate in Switzerland. Flanked by round towers, the gateway and its tent roof of a later date soar up so decidedly that the whole structure can be called a gate-tower. The Madonna and two apostles under the baldachins above the arch of the gateway are evidence of the municipal desire for representation in a religious form. The small gateway in front with the decorated frieze of battlements and the two figures bearing coats of arms was added by Jakob Sarbach in 1473.

ROSTOCK, KRÖPELIN GATE

In comparison with the massive, broad silhouette of the Holsten Gate in Lübeck, the square tower of the Kröpelin Gate in the seaport of Rostock is an example of another typical aspect of Gothic brick architecture, the urge to achieve great heights. There is hardly any decoration on the main part of this outstanding town gate, erected in the first half of the 15th century, but to make up for this it has a profusion of gables with blind windows in white plaster. There once was a projecting walk around it. Although the modern architecture of the Warnow Hotel in the background belongs to quite another epoch, both structures have in common a clear, cubic approach, deriving their vitality from the surface structure of the walls.

LÜBECK, HOLSTEN GATE

Lübeck, a free city of the Reich from 1226 to 1937, was the center of the most powerful union of cities of the Middle Ages, the Hanseatic League. It possesses the most splendid gateway of Northern Europe, the Holsten Gate.

The Holsten Gate was erected by Hinrich Helmstede between 1467 and 1477, a time when the power of the Hanseatic League was already declining. This monumental structure has a uniform facade on the side facing the city, while on the other side the two towers flanking the gateway jut out like bastions with their conical roofs, a manifestation of the city's former power.

The broad outline of the building is articulated by rows of windows and blind arches, and by the interplay of red brick and glazed tiles. There is little use of ornamentation; it is the effect of the massive, original parts of the structure which dominates the overall impression. Only the top row of blind arches and the central gable were renewed in 1863.

FRANKFORT-ON-THE-MAIN, ESCHENHEIM TOWER

With the traffic of the big city surging around it, the imposing Eschenheim Tower stands as one of the few surviving parts of the mighty town fortifications built on the northern promenade ring in Frankfort on the banks of the Main. Begun by Master Mengoz in 1400 and continued until 1428 by Madern Gertener, its artistry consists mainly in the combination of the simple round tower with the stimulating profusion of little projecting towers, corbels, and battlements, this being a typical characteristic of the Late Gothic Period. Often in danger during the 19th century of being razed as an obstacle to traffic —a fate suffered by most of the town gates of the Middle Ages—it now stands on a traffic island amidst new surroundings.

SPEYER, ALTPÖRTEL

In the old imperial city of Speyer on the Rhine, there is one of the finest city gateway-towers of the Federal Republic of Germany, known as the Altpörtel. The massive tower of smooth stone dates from the Late Romanesque Period (*c.* 1240) and consequently, apart from the blind arches, has no ornamentation on the side facing the town. The severe, simple beauty of this structure is not spoiled either by the tracery parapet of the upper gallery, added in 1514, or by the Renaissance turrets on the high conical roof.

79

STENDAL, ÜNGLINGER GATE

The use of the constructional material for decoration in Gothic architecture is shown at its finest in the Unglinger Gate, a gateway in the town of Stendal in Altmark. The rectangular gate-tower with its circular upper section was erected about 1440. Without detriment to its defensive qualities, it was lavishly decorated with white-plaster blind windows, ornamental friezes, and glazed tiles. The overhanging towers and the richly articulated battlements have an almost toylike air about them. They are evidence of an artistic advance of a very high order in an epoch which marks the end of the building of town gates. The houses in the background, dating from the 18th and 19th centuries, convey an idea of the original scale, convincingly demonstrating the desire for collective security.

NEUBRANDENBURG, TREPTOW GATE

The splendid Treptow Gate in Neubrandenburg, dating from the 15th century, represents a new variation of the fortified gateway. This kind of double gateway offered more protection against firearms. The lower outer gate, with the characteristic decoration of molded brick and red-and-white color contrasts, is extended over the moat and linked by walls to the higher inner gate. Should the enemy succeed in penetrating the outer gate, he found himself in the confined space of the "zwinger," as it was called, exposed to devastating fire from two sides. At the inner gate, the portcullis between the two staircase towers barred the way to the town. Here, too, it will be noticed that the pronounced pleasure in ornamentation of the Late Gothic Period accompanied the development of the military fortifications.

WARSAW, BARBICAN

The most advanced form of medieval town gate was the layout in which the barbican was extended like a bridgehead over the moat with the task of absorbing the initial attack. This example from Warsaw, reconstructed true to historical detail between 1950 and 1954 (it suffered great damage in the Second World War), has a typical semicircular ground plan, guaranteeing a maximum angle of fire. In the outer part, which is not covered by a roof, the defending marksmen were accommodated in casementlike rooms linked by communication gangways. Like many other gateways in Eastern Europe, the gate in Warsaw from the 16th century does not have any decoration.

TORUN, BRIDGE GATE

The Mostava bridge gate, a massive structure with rounded corners and hardly any decoration, was one of five gates which closed off the old town of Torun from the Vistula River and at the same time provided access to the quays. The portcullis was located in the lower part of the wall, above the pointed arch of the gateway. The gate was built in the time when the town was controlled by the German Knights of the Cross, whose castle in Torun was razed to the ground by the victorious Poles in 1454.

GDANSK, CRANE GATE

In addition to defense, the crane gate built in 1411 on the banks of the Motlava in Gdansk has an unusual function. In the higher central part, which completely dominates the semicircular towers projecting at the corners, there is a treadmill which could be used for unloading ships. This historic building, which was rebuilt after World War II, now accommodates the Sea Museum.

CAHORS, PONT VALENTRÉ
In the French department of Lot, on the river of
the same name, lies the episcopal town of Cahors
with its strongly fortified bridge, Pont Valentré.
This bridge, begun in 1308 as an important link
in communications protected by three rectangular
gatetowers, spans the river with six pointed arches.

AVIGNON, PONT SAINT-BÉNÉZET
One of the early medieval stone bridges, the Saint-
Bénézet bridge in the town of Avignon on the
Rhône was built between 1177 and 1185, and destroyed in 1669. It took its name from the Chapel
consecrated to St. Bénézet which stood on one of
the pillars of the bridge. The picture shows the
ruins of this structure, which no doubt was also
used as a bastion.

ROTHENBURG, MARKUS TOWER
This view of the Markus Tower and the Röder
Arch in the center of Rothenburg ob der Tauber
gives a good idea of a German town in the Middle
Ages. No importance is attached to symmetry. The
small houses hug the fortifications, making an
attractive sight, but the practical point of this in
the past was to make it difficult for the enemy to
survey the lay of the land and to advance in a
straight line. The ridge turret and the clock on
the gate-tower date from the Renaissance.

Bautzen, Alte Wasserkunst

BAUTZEN, ALTE WASSERKUNST

High above the Spree River, built on craggy rocks, there is the Alte Wasserkunst in Bautzen. Together with the church of St. Michael behind it, it forms a vigorous and impressive group. This 160-foot-high tower, which is of great technical interest, was built by Wenzel Röhrscheidt for the water supply system. As long ago as 1496, running water was brought into the town by a scoop-wheel housed in a wooden tower.

The "Alte Wasserkunst," built in 1558 and of vital importance for the town, was equipped with a low-slung covered walk and a parapet. The lower part is still in use for the water supply, while in the upper rooms there is a museum. Stellar vaulting can be seen in the seven-storied interior, a typical form of vaulting during the Late Gothic Period.

LINDAU, THIEF'S TOWER AND TOWER OF ST. PETER'S CHURCH

Very picturesque is this group of towers from Lindau which is built on an island in Lake Constance. In the foreground, there is the simple rectangular tower of St. Peter's Church, dating from the 8th century; behind it, to the left, is the round Thief's Tower of the old town wall with its turret towers. Its core originates from a watch tower erected by the Romans, who maintained a camp on the strategically well-placed island.

*Lindau, Thief's Tower and Tower of
St. Peter's Church*

AUGSBURG, WATER TOWERS AND RED GATE

Most of the medieval town gates of Augsburg were "modernized" at the beginning of the 17th century by Elias Holl, the distinguished German architect of the Renaissance. The Red Gate, reconstructed in 1622, was articulated in the upper story by horizontal strips, but this did not destroy the heavy, compact massiveness of the old gate. The overall impression remains medieval and picturesque with the water towers, built at a later date, in the background.

PRAGUE, OLD TOWN TOWER OF CHARLES BRIDGE

One of Europe's most beautiful bridges is the Charles Bridge in Prague, commissioned by Charles IV and built by Peter Parler of Gmünd in the years after 1357. It is 1,700 feet long, spans the Vltava with 16 arches, and has gateways for defense at its ends. The decoration is particularly magnificent on the Old Town gate-tower. As with a triumphal portal, on the side facing the town there are statues of the two royal patrons, Charles IV and Wenceslaus IV, and of the saints Adalbert, Veit, and Sigismund in an elaborate blind panel system of decoration in typical Late Gothic forms. The outstanding quality of the sculptured ornamentation makes this simple tower one of the most artistically significant towers of Europe.

LISBON, TOWER OF BELÉM

At the mouth of the Tejo and once isolated on a rocky island, there is a magnificently decorated citadel with the Tower of Belém (Bethlehem). It was erected by the architect Francisco de Arrunda between 1515 and 1521, on the orders of King Manuel I, as a defense for the mighty port of Lisbon. One of the symbols of Portugal, it is also one of the most beautiful fortified towers of Europe. The

profusion of ornamental forms, oriels, and turrets is not only based on Moorish traditions but also includes elements of style from India, which had been rediscovered at this time.

As in Spain, the escutcheons decorated with crosses (the sign of the Order of Christ) on the battlements demonstrate the close links between the monarchy and the Church, which used this citadel as a symbol of their combined power in addition to its function of defense. Vasco da Gama, discoverer of the sea route to India, set out on his adventurous voyage from here. For a long time, the tower's lower level served as a prison.

FLORENCE, PALAZZO VECCHIO

Even before the triumph of bourgeois self-assurance in the Renaissance, the town hall was the most important building for the display of municipal power. In this connection, it is noteworthy that in Italy, as opposed to France and Germany, the urge to achieve great heights for purposes of representation was expressed not in ecclesiastical architecture but in this area of secular architecture. In Florence, the leading city of this new age, Dante in 1314 was able to witness the completion of the Palazzo Vecchio, begun by Arnolfo di Cambio in 1298. With its asymmetrically placed tower, the structure still looks like a fortress and, indeed, in the stormy history of Florence, this was the function it often enough performed. The airy belfry, which is more relaxed in style and is over 300 feet high, was not added until the 15th century.

SIENA, PALAZZO PUBLICO
AND TORRE DEL MANGIA

In competition with Florence, the citizens of Siena built a fine municipal palace on the Piazza del Campo between 1282 and 1305 and, as a symbol of their power, added the Torre del Mangia to it between 1325 and 1345. With its height of 325 feet,

Lisbon, Tower of Belém
Florence, Palazzo Vecchio

Siena, Palazzo Publico and Torre del Mangia

the tower is one of the highest in Italy. The richly articulated top part, with the battlements and belfry, make the severe vertical lines of the slim body of the tower ring out like a free chord.

BOLOGNA, ASINELLI AND GARISENDA

The leaning towers of Bologna are the symbol of the city, and are called Asinelli and Garisenda from the names of the noble families who had them built about 1200. Family towers such as these were to be found in many Italian towns; in Bologna alone there were 200. The older Garisenda Tower is 157 feet high, while the Asinelli Tower reaches a height of more than 320 feet. The latter is already four feet off the perpendicular at the top. The completely plain and clear-cut towers, one of which was compared by Dante to the giant Antaeus, achieve their monumental effect solely by their economy of form.

SAN GIMIGNANO, FAMILY TOWERS

Not far from Siena is the mountain town of San Gimignano, which conveys an almost unaltered impression of a medieval town torn by violent feuds among the aristocracy. Of the 56 family towers which performed the function of the keep of a knightly castle within the town walls, 13 still stand in a very confined space. They are an imposing symbol of the insistent need for defense in the 12th and 13th centuries, which did not yet link the self-assurance evident here with the humanist spirit of the Renaissance. In Florence, more than 100 of such towers threatened to stifle the town and be a hindrance to civil life. Here, however, the merchants forced them to be limited in height to 50 ells, a circumstance which considerably stimulated the building of palazzi by the aristocracy.

YPRES, CLOTH HALL

The might and rank of the old Flemish town of Ypres is proclaimed by the Cloth Hall, completed in 1357. This is an ornate, three-story trade and warehouse building with a 230-foot-high belfry dating from the 13th century (the belfry was reconstructed after being destroyed in the First World War).

Certain types of watch towers and fortified towers which had originated in castle architecture were subsequently used as a pattern in secular buildings, such as the Italian town hall and family towers. These secular structures reached noteworthy heights and were of a particularly elaborate design during the Late Gothic Period in the wealthy Low Countries. In contrast to Italy, however, the belfries of Flanders are rendered less severe by rows of windows and Gothic decoration.

TORUN, TOWN HALL

With its 344-foot-high corner tower, which was originally part of the older building begun in 1259, the town hall of Torun has a massive and defiant air. Resembling a castle of the Teutonic Knights, it was not only the seat of the city administration and judiciary but also contained shops and meat and bread stalls. The corner turrets and central gables of this mighty rectangular structure were added in the 17th century.

ALTENBURG, TOWN HALL

Although the town hall in Altenburg, which was built between 1562 and 1564 according to plans drawn up by Nikolaus Gromann, belongs to the Renaissance period, the ensemble of an ostentatious tower and an administrative building is evidence of the continuing tradition of the Middle Ages (Torun). Yet the effect of this piece of architecture of the new period is more refreshing. The slim, octagonal staircase tower with the airy lan-

tern at the top is flanked by two richly decorated oriels at the main front. It soars into the air, giving a cheerful and well-balanced impression with only the dominating tower-element still recalling the Gothic Period.

PRAGUE, CLOCK TOWER OF THE OLD TOWN TOWN HALL

A special tourist attraction is Prague's Great Clock of the Old Town Hall Tower, built in the 14th century. This simple tower, which was built on Romanesque foundations, provides a fine view of the Old Town. The part of the tower housing the astronomical clock designed by Master Hanuš z Ruže was added about 1480.

The clock was rebuilt in 1860, and a calendar was painted on it by Manes. At the stroke of the hour, a cock crows and the apostles emerge from the apertures at the top; underneath, framed by delicate Late Gothic ornamentation, the change of the planets, months, and years is indicated. The spirit of the Renaissance is already apparent in the knowledge and inventive genius displayed here.

VENICE, CLOCK TOWER

The clock tower, erected between 1496 and 1499, is on the northern side of the famous St. Mark's Square in Venice. Its articulation is fully integrated with the Renaissance facade of the Palace and its tower character is revealed only by the story rising above the structure, topped by the two figures by Paolo Secin (1497) which strike the hours. With its distinct, well-proportioned lines and the colored mosaic of the top story, it is a genuine child of the Italian Renaissance, and specifically of the Venetian kind. The lion of St. Mark, the heraldic animal of Venice, lends the clock tower a significant symbolic quality.

PADUA, CLOCK TOWER
The clock tower of Padua is clearly a symbol of temporal power. Added to the Palazzo del Capitanio in 1532 by Falconetto, it is open like a triumphal arch at the bottom and provided with a guard room at the top, above the clock. Over the gateway is the lion, the sign of Venetian sovereignty. This explains the triumphal character of this tower, since Padua was conquered by the Republic of Venice in 1406 and was subsequently ruled by a Venetian governor in the Palazzo del Capitanio.

BERNE, ZEITGLOCKENTURM
The famous striking-clock tower in Berne was originally a fortified town gate, erected by Kuno von Bubenberg in 1191. With the Renaissance, it largely ceased to function as such and was given a new facade in 1530. At the same time, a huge clock movement by the Nuremberg clockmaker Caspar Brunner was also installed. All other clocks in the town were set by this one. This tower and its opposite number in the Marktgasse, the Käfigturm, mark the limits of one of the loveliest street areas in Europe.

TROGIR, CLOCK TOWER
In the Yugoslav town of Trogir, too, a fortified tower was converted into a clock tower at the time of the Renaissance. It has a modestly decorated facade.

GRAZ, CLOCK TOWER
This very original little clock tower on the Schlossberg at Graz was likewise once a fortified Gothic tower. Between 1560 and 1570, it was given the brattice and the clock; its great dial of over 16 feet in diameter can be seen from far away.

VENICE, SCALA MINELLI
In the courtyard of the Palazzo Minelli in Venice
is the Scala Minelli, a spiral-staircase tower built
by Giovanni Candi about 1490. Though still basi-
cally Gothic in design, it has left the Middle Ages
far behind with its open arcades, which give it a
light and elegant appearance. Venice once had
more of these staircase towers, but with the advance
of the Renaissance, which preferred horizontal
articulation to any diagonal form, they ceased to
be built and most of the existing ones were demolished.

MEISSEN, STAIRCASE TOWER OF THE
ALBRECHTSBURG
The Albrechtsburg at Meissen was begun in 1471
by Arnold von Westphalen. With its staircase tower or "Grosser Wendelstein," it is the earliest
example in Germany of the transition from the
massive fortified castle of the Middle Ages to the
ostentatious palace. The tower is still dominated
by Late Gothic features, yet the wall has wide
apertures in it and the horizontal areas of the
loggia parapets soften the verticality. This feature
of the ostentatious staircase tower set in front of
the main structure was to prove very popular in
later years. The view of the interior with the fluted
ribs, the ribbed vaulting, and the spiral handrail
still shows Late Gothic influence.

TORGAU, STAIRCASE TOWER
OF THE HARTENFELS PALACE
A few decades after the building of the castle at
Meissen, Konrad Krebs added a splendid spiral-
staircase tower to the Johann Friedrich Wing of
Hartenfels Palace between 1533 and 1536. The
structure projects far in front of the rest of the
building and is hardly recognizable as a tower. Although designed in the style of the Early Renaissance, it still recalls the Gothic Period in such

Meissen, Staircase Tower of the Albrechtsburg

Meissen, Staircase Tower of the Albrechtsburg

Torgau, Staircase Tower of the Hartenfels Palace

Rothenburg, Hegereiterhaus
Blois, Staircase Tower of the Château

details as the convolution of the staircase and the skeletonlike construction. Nevertheless, the unusual accentuation of the entrance area, which is reinforced by its symmetrical position and the two outside staircases, anticipates the mighty interior staircases of Baroque palaces. The architect was probably familiar with similar structures in France.

ROTHENBURG, HEGEREITERHAUS

Many other buildings featured a spiral staircase but on a much simplified scale. A fine example is the massive tower of the Hegereiterhaus, as it is called, in the courtyard of the medieval infirmary of Rothenburg. Begun in 1591, the small tower is crowned by an airy lantern.

BLOIS, STAIRCASE TOWER OF THE CHÂTEAU

Of the many châteaux along the Loire in which the transition to the Renaissance style can be seen, that at Blois, with its "grand escalier," has the finest 16th-century staircase tower of France. Built between 1530 and 1540, it does not attain the height of the ridge of the main structure, but it does extend above the cornice and is richly decorated. The vertical spacing of the staircase flights roughly corresponds to the articulation of the facade, where the stress is completely on horizontality. This explains why the spiral/diagonal feature of Gothic style was abandoned when the Renaissance became firmly established, and why the staircase tower had to yield to the interior staircase.

Poznan, Town Hall Tower
Copenhagen, Exchange

POZNAN, TOWN HALL TOWER

The town hall of Poznan, rebuilt after World War II, is one of the most beautiful in Poland. It was built, following a fire in the middle of the 16th century, by the Italian architect Giovanni Gianbattista Quadro on what could still be used of the old Gothic town hall. It was based on North Italian models. Quadro also raised the Gothic tower which, when the top was added in 1783, reached a height of over 200 feet.

COPENHAGEN, EXCHANGE

Scarcely more than a ridge turret but of very original design is the tower of the Exchange in Copenhagen. It was built in the 17th century in the then popular Flemish-Dutch style with its characteristic alternation of brick and stone masonry. The Exchange symbolizes the rise of bourgeois power in the maritime state of Denmark. The incredible spire above the lantern, consisting of four dragon tails twisted like a rope, is an unmistakable landmark on this long, low building at the waterfront. The use of nonarchitectural forms such as this is evidence of a frivolous trait which was expressed in particular during the Baroque Period, when the tower no longer played any significant role.

AMSTERDAM, MONTALBAAN TOWER

Visible from far as a landmark and clock tower is the 17th-century Montalbaan Tower on the picturesque Gracht Oude Schans. Located directly at the port mouth of Amsterdam, it dates from the time when the city was still a center of world trade. The round, fortresslike lower part is somewhat unexpectedly crowned by a light Baroque superstructure which, in silhouette, looks like a steep, conical roof.

AMSTERDAM, TOWER OF THE ZUIDERKERK

Obviously a continuation of Gothic ecclesiastical architecture, Dutch churches of the Baroque period have very high and ornate bell towers. This development was certainly due to Dutch Protestantism following the war with Catholic Spain. The Zuiderkerk in Amsterdam, built by Hendrik de Keyser between 1603 and 1614, specifically demonstrates this by the design of its clock tower. With its stepped construction—not extending upward without interruption as in the Gothic style—this structure reflects the influence of Classic and Baroque forms. As in many other towers of the Netherlands, there is a fine peal of bells in the lantern.

HOORN, HARBOR TOWER

During the golden age of the Dutch merchant marine, the trading company of the town of Hoorn on the Zuiderzee erected a towerlike building with a ridge turret crowned by two airy lanterns. Typically Dutch is the use of stone banding to give a lively contrast with the brick masonry of the rest of the structure. The clock, with its various chimes, is a reminder of the spirit of commerce.

SOPRON, TOWN TOWER

Like many other medieval towers, the 200-foot-high town tower of Sopron on Lake Neusiedel was raised during the Renaissance and Baroque periods and made more ornate by the addition of a portal, an observation gallery halfway up, and an alien crown. The tower then served as a watch-tower from which fires in the surrounding areas could be detected. Today, it shares the fate of most of these towers—it has become a lookout post for tourists.

DRESDEN, CATHOLIC COURT CHURCH

The revival of the Gothic tower tradition in German Baroque architecture is best exemplified by the Catholic Court Church in Dresden. The slim main tower—266 feet high, its pierced, skeleton-like stories becoming smaller with increasing height—recalls the silhouette of a Gothic spire. Even the Italian architect Gaetano Chiaveri, who laid the foundation stone for this ornate Court Church of Augustus II in 1739, had to yield to this tradition. The German architects who followed him, S. Wetzel, J.C. Knoeffel, and J.H. Schwartze, increased the height of the tower, which was completed in 1755. The reason for this and also for the tower's unusual position on the northeast side was the endeavor to make it visible from the Elbe and from the new district of Dresden.

VERONA, PORTA STUPA (PORTA PALIO)

The development of firearms and the new intellectual climate of the Renaissance led to the disappearance in the 16th century of the town gate with its stress on towers. In its place emerged the low fortified gate in strict Renaissance forms. An excellent example of this type, in which ostentation is not abandoned but expressed in a new form akin to the triumphal arch, was created by the Italian Michele Sanmicheli in 1557 with his Porta Stupa in Verona. The antique elements of column, gable, and entablature with metope frieze are economically and neatly combined in a facade which, with its compact proportions and rustic work, cannot but help look like a fortress.

GDANSK, HIGH GATE

The High Gate, built between 1574 and 1576 during the Renaissance, and the medieval gate behind it form a fine architectural group. They also form a single unit from the military point of view, since in the early 16th century gun loops were

made in the walls on the sixth and seventh floors for the artillery; the High Gate, with its resemblance to a triumphal arch, originally had drawbridges to protect the entrances. The complex also includes the Golden Gate, seen in the background. On the splendid attic part of the High Gate are the old coats of arms of Poland, Prussia, and Danzig.

SZCZECIN, HARBOR GATE

Very heavy and massive in appearance is the Harbor Gate of Szczecin, which was erected in 1725 and is an example of the fortified Baroque gate. However, the elaborate trophy group on the attic and the triumphant genii over the arch, the work of the sculptor Damast of Berlin, is evidence of the priority of ostentation over defense. On the attic there is a relief of the god of the waters.

LISBON, TRIUMPHAL GATE
ON PRAÇA DO COMMERCIO

The idea of the triumph of royal power was interpreted in an artistically significant form during the Baroque period—especially in the royal residences of Europe—by reviving the Roman triumphal arch. Thus, after the earthquake of 1755, Lisbon received a mighty triumphal arch dividing the famous Praça do Commercio (Square of Commerce) and at the same time forming an imposing boundary mark at the junction with the Rua Augusta. The allegorical group above the panel with the Portuguese coat of arms is dedicated to the illustrious deeds of past heroes.

Montpellier, Triumphal Arch of Louis XIV

Innsbruck, Triumphal Portal

Paris, Arc de Triomphe de l'Etoile

MONTPELLIER, TRIUMPHAL ARCH OF LOUIS XIV

An impressive Arc de Triomphe, almost 50 feet in height, was erected in honor of Louis XIV in Montpellier in 1691. It likewise forms an imposing limit to a street. In contrast to the usual Baroque exuberance, however, this arch with its rich decoration of symbolic accessories is of severe and simple design, an example of classically restrained Baroque in France.

INNSBRUCK, TRIUMPHAL PORTAL

On the occasion of the entry of the Empress Maria Theresa and her consort Franz I in 1765, a triple-arched triumphal gate was erected on the main arterial road leading into the new area of Innsbruck. It was decorated with the reliefs of Austrian princes. The rather severe composition and reserved ornamentation place this structure in the style of Louis XVI (rococo), in whose time a classical trend dominated the end of the Baroque period.

PARIS, ARC DE TRIOMPHE DE L'ETOILE

After Napoleon's defeat of the Prussians and Austrians in 1806, he had the biggest triumphal arch of Europe erected on the Champs Elysées in Paris to immortalize his fame. After the plans of Jean François Chalgrin, its dimensions were 148 feet high, 164 feet wide, and 72 feet deep. This severely classical arch is three times the size of the Arch of Titus in Rome, on which it was modeled. Napoleon intentionally continued the traditions of structures from the Roman Empire in order to lend historical justification to his empire, which was also based on conquests.

The project was not completed, however, until 1837, 22 years after Napoleon's banishment to the island of St. Helena, and he did not live to see it. The reliefs around the arch record his victories,

while the vigorous high reliefs of the march of the volunteers of 1792, carved by François Rude between 1832 and 1836, recall the great days of the French Revolution.

LENINGRAD, GATEWAY-TOWER OF THE ADMIRALTY

An unusual gateway-tower design in the architectural style of Russian Classicism is that of the Admiralty Tower of Leningrad. Sakharov, who built the Admiralty complex between 1806 and 1820, erected this triumphal tower high above the long facade of the Admiralty as a conspicuous symbol of Russia's new sea power. This verticality, which is alien to Classicism and is enormously enhanced by the needlelike tip, combines the idea of the triumphal arch with the concept of the obelisk in a novel manner.

BERLIN, BRANDENBURG GATE

The Brandenburg Gate, based on the Propylaea of the Acropolis and erected by Karl Gotthard Langhans between 1788 and 1791, is the symbol of Berlin. The solemn Doric front of the lofty center section is flanked by two low temples with rooms for the guard, and resembles a courtyard of honor. This architecture, which follows in the triumphal tradition, is simple, severe, and well-balanced in all its component parts. The quadriga with the goddess Victoria was designed by Gottfried Schadow and was placed on the Gate as the crowning feature in 1794. Badly damaged during the Second World War, it was subsequently restored.

DRESDEN, CROWN GATE OF THE ZWINGER

The magnificent Crown Gate (Kronentor) of the Zwinger at Dresden was built between 1711 and 1728 by Daniel Pöppelmann and ornamented with statues by Balthasar Permoser. It exudes the

atmosphere of the highly sophisticated court life of the Late Baroque Period. The extravagant profusion of statues, ornamentation, and architecture blend together to produce a cheerful masterpiece of royal ostentation, symbolized by the four heraldic eagles and the crown on top.

MUNICH, PROPYLAEA

Even the name of the Propylaea in Munich, designed by Leo von Klenze and built between 1848 and 1862 at the command of the King of Bavaria, indicates its derivation from the Greek model. Yet the small portico with the heavy, massive towers, set back on either side, does not look very Greek. Indeed, in its distant and remote majesty, it rather resembles the facade of an Egyptian temple with its pylons. The fusion of two types of architecture here may be considered as evidence, however, that since the period of Classicism originality could no longer be obtained, despite the many triumphal gates that continued to be erected. The architectural justification for the gate had ceased to exist.

LEIPZIG, ENTRANCE TO THE TECHNICAL FAIR

The design of the entrances to the Technical Fair in Leipzig, the famous venue of international fairs, can be regarded as a modern way of accentuating the entrance area of socially significant complexes. Admittedly, such a design is far removed from the concept of the gateway. Two steel frames, about 82 feet high and sheathed in aluminum, stand in the form of a superimposed double "M." This serves as an easily remembered symbol for "Muster-Messe," the German expression for "sample-fair," and indicates the nature of the site from far away.

Löbauer Berg, Observation Tower

BERLIN, ROTES RATHAUS

The "Red City Hall"—so named after its red-brick masonry—was built by Waesemann between 1861 and 1869. It is a typical example of a return to the historical designs of the past, and the magnificent clock tower in the center of the facade is based on the towers of Laon Cathedral.

LÖBAUER BERG, OBSERVATION TOWER

On the 1,444-foot-high peak of this mountain in Upper Lusatia, there is the only remaining cast-iron observation tower in Europe. It was erected in 1854 and is 82 feet high. Despite the then novel building material, which was soon to prove a new stimulus for architecture, the ornate minaretlike tower here, endowed by a master baker of Löbau, is totally eclectic in character. The view of the interior with its confusing complexity shows that at this time the aesthetic qualities of iron structures were not fully appreciated, and the forms and filigree work customary in stonemasonry were merely reproduced in the new material.

LONDON, HOUSES OF PARLIAMENT

With the development of the middle class and industry, the 19th century made many new demands on architectural forms. The tower, at first in an eclectic form, achieved new significance. Thus the Houses of Parliament, designed by Sir Charles Barry and built between 1840 and 1852 along the Thames in London, were given a neo-Gothic facade and three towers. One of these was the famous Big Ben. This 318-foot-high clock tower is the symbol of London, and the chime of its bells is known throughout the world.

LONDON, TOWER BRIDGE

Not only industry but also the very much heavier traffic of the 19th century needed towers. The engineers concerned were not at all inclined to dispense with ornamentation simply because the towers were primarily intended to serve a functional purpose. This point is demonstrated by the illustration of the famous Tower Bridge in London, built between 1886 and 1894. It represents a strange amalgamation of the steel bridge structures of modern times and the stone edifices of the past: the bridge towers use the medieval principle of the drawbridge to allow large ships to pass through underneath the bridge.

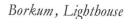

BORKUM, LIGHTHOUSE
The lighthouse on the East Frisian island of Borkum, dating from the second half of the 19th century, rises up to the sky like a slim minaret. With its bright red color, it serves as an aid to navigation during daylight as well. Towers of this kind were not usually designed with any particular aesthetic considerations in mind. They merely had to be high enough and have a firm location—which, on sandy ground, can be achieved by the use of a socket foundation base. Set against a barren background, this tower is a fascinating sight.

PARIS, EIFFEL TOWER
This was the sensation of the Paris International Exposition of 1889—the much-admired and much-maligned steel tower of the French engineer Alexandre Gustave Eiffel. Reaching a height of almost a thousand feet, it set a new record and, although of no practical usefulness, was intended as a symbol of the glory of France, which contributed 6.5 million gold francs for its construction. It was also intended as a triumph of engineering for the man who used the despised material, steel, to achieve such a dizzy height.

When the project was first proposed, well-known French artists protested against the unnecessary and "monstrous" Eiffel Tower (Maupassant called it an "atrocity of iron"). Despite the use it made of such traditional forms as the arch, the triumphal gate, and the obelisk, it was too much for the conventional views and opinions of the time. As an airy skeleton structure, it was assembled in 17 months from 12,000 component parts; 2.8 million rivets hold it together, it weighs 7,500 tons, and has a span of 312 feet.

But of more importance than the new records in the time of construction, the dimensions, and the quantities of material used, was its invisible but revolutionary significance for future tower design.

Paris, Eiffel Tower

The advance to such a great height with the new material, steel, was also an advance in new constructional techniques and scientific findings. In view of the very limited time available for the project, Eiffel was obliged to plan all phases of construction in advance, using a kind of critical path technique. He had to carry out investigations with a wind tunnel in his own laboratory to determine the magnitude of the aerodynamic load on the tower. For further investigations, he had a small laboratory built at a height of over 900 feet. New aspects appeared in the architect's profession and Eiffel had to be not only an artist but, more than before, a statics expert, scientist, economist, and organizer.

Not to be forgotten, either, is the courage of those nameless steel erectors who, exposed to the full force of the wind at so great a height and largely unprotected by safety measures, successfully completed the work. And there was not a single fatal accident. These daring men were known as "chimney sweeps" to their colleagues.

Together with the Leaning Tower of Pisa, the Eiffel Tower is the most famous tower in the world. A good year after its construction, its full cost was recovered from the money paid by sightseers. Whereas the other structures of the Exposition of 1889 have long since disappeared, the Eiffel Tower has become the center of an imposing park, and it is today the symbol of Paris. In the past, the only function of the tower was to provide a view of over 90 miles, but now a 59-foot-high mast has been added to it and it also serves as a television tower. In 1957, its twin brother was built in Tokyo with a height of 1,092 feet. But the fact of greatest importance is that the Eiffel Tower was the first of a wide-ranging family of steel skeleton towers which can be found in large numbers all over the world.

COPENHAGEN, CITY HALL

The breakthrough to modern architecture at the beginning of the 20th century was certainly anticipated by developments in engineering, and new materials such as steel and concrete. Nonetheless, the contribution of architects aware of their responsibility and rejecting ornate and derivative conventions was still needed to complete it. The tower of the city hall in Copenhagen, which recalls the towers of the Italian palazzi, is a simple, rectangular structure of brick, and thus an important contribution to the aesthetics of tower design. It was built by the Dane Martin Myrop between 1893 and 1903.

STUTTGART, RAILWAY STATION

The tower of the New Railway Station in Stuttgart, the work of Paul Bonatz and Eugen Friedrich Scheler between 1914 and 1927, illustrates the last consequence of cubic simplification. This structure, with rustic work and windows as its only articulation, fits in splendidly with the ensemble of other buildings which follow the same principles and thus accentuate the striking impression of the tower as an imposing high point.

RIGA, RAILWAY STATION

The clock tower of the railway station in Riga, built a few years ago, utilizes the new possiblities in the accentuation of verticality. This slender and simple structure, articulated only by four dark vertical bands on the facade, has a severely beautiful air about it.

DARMSTADT, HOCHZEITSTURM

In an atmosphere of fresh ideas, the Viennese architect Josef Maria Olbrich was able to build the avant-gardist Hochzeitsturm (wedding tower) on the Mathildenhöhe in Darmstadt between 1905 and 1908 for the exhibition building of the Secession movement. The severe walls of this clinker tower

Stuttgart, Railway Station

Riga, Railway Station

Darmstadt, Hochzeitsturm

have been given a rhythmic liveliness by asymmetrical window apertures. Although it still recalls Gothic gables, the treatment of the roof zone is original. Locally, this best-known work of Olbrich has won the name of "five-finger tower."

POTSDAM, EINSTEIN TOWER

The 20th century brought not only a strict cubic form of tower but also dynamic forms, full of fantasy, which were made possible by the invention of reinforced concrete. With the Einstein Tower, the observatory he built in Potsdam in 1921, Erich Mendelsohn has given an impressive demonstration of the tremendous potential of this material, and of a new approach to aesthetics in tower design. Mendelsohn swept away all previous concepts with this lively, aerodynamic form, reminiscent of the armored turret of a battleship. He was, of course, under the impact not only of Jugendstil and Expressionism but also of the deeply moving experience of the First World War.

BERLIN (WEST), KAISER FRIEDRICH MEMORIAL CHURCH

An example of the great variety of forms in modern ecclesiastical architecture is the bell tower of the Kaiser Friedrich Memorial Church, built by Ludwig Lemmer in West Berlin in 1955–1956. It conveys an idea of how modern reinforced concrete can be shaped for a solemn purpose. The spiral staircase visible in the framework tower next to the nave, where the resemblance to the Gothic style is not accidental, is supported in its airy lightness by disciplined vertical strips, an original contrast of spiral and linear elements in a dynamic upward movement. But the residential skyscrapers surrounding the clock tower are higher. Thus, in contrast to the Middle Ages, when the highest towers were those of the churches, the church tower has yielded its dominant architectural position to functional buildings.

HELSINKI, TOWER OF THE OLYMPIC STADIUM

Modern sports complexes, mostly low structures and areas, often possess an imposing bell and clock tower as the only dominant feature. For the Olympic Games in Helsinki, a reinforced concrete tower, almost 240 feet in height, was erected at the stadium. On one side, as a lively contrast to the unarticulated surface areas, it was given a projecting staircase with semicircular balconies. This tower is one of the highest and most beautiful in Finland, which had not been noted for towers in the past.

BUCHENWALD, BELL TOWER

As a lasting memorial to the 56,000 dead from 18 nations and to the self-liberation of the surviving prisoners in the Nazi concentration camp of Buchenwald, a severe and solemn memorial tower of stone was erected on the Ettersberg near Weimar between 1954 and 1958. It forms a landmark as part of a vast complex on the plateau. The upper part, which is stepped in two stages and is articulated by rows of pillars, reveals classicistic influence and rises like a restrained but triumphant chord above the heavy and massive lower section. In front of the tower is Fritz Cremer's monumental bronze group of the prisoners freeing themselves.

CONSTANŢA, LIGHTHOUSE

The elegantly ascending lighthouse of the Rumanian port of Constanţa is an excellent example of how reinforced concrete can be used for the creation of towers of original design, even when the tower is composed of simple functional structures. The lighthouse is a dynamic combination of two basic shapes—the upturned pyramid of the lantern with its facetlike surface is placed in an offset position on the tip of the slender concrete tower, which rises like an obelisk.

Buchenwald, Bell Tower

ROTTERDAM, EUROMAST

In the city of Rotterdam, badly damaged in World War II, there is the Euromast, one of the most original of the modern observation towers of Europe. The 390-foot-high tower consists largely of a hollow reinforced-concrete cylinder, 30 feet in diameter. At a height of 328 feet, it has an asymmetrical steel cage, the three levels of which accommodate a café, a bar, a post office, service rooms, and the observation platform. The elegant design, resembling the superstructure of a modern ocean liner, illustrates that the illusion of a structure apparently hanging weightless in the air is an important aspect of modern tower architecture. At 105 feet, a complete ship's bridge has been installed as a tourist attraction.

LONDON, COMMUNICATIONS
AND OBSERVATION TOWER (GPO TOWER)

The silhouette of London is dominated, since 1965, by the 620-foot-high communications and observation tower of the GPO. The hollow core of reinforced concrete, 580 feet high and only 22 feet in diameter, is encircled by 29 glazed floors for radio and communications equipment up to a height of 350 feet. This conveys the impression of a slender office skyscraper. Other observation galleries then follow like superimposed discs, a 40-foot-high aerial mast marking the tip of the tower. The use of areas of colored glass is another new approach to tower design.

MOSCOW, TELEVISION TOWER

With its height of 1,763 feet, Moscow's television tower is still the highest building in the world, since the TV masts in Fargo, North Dakota, which are 2,062 and 2,072 feet high, are not works of architecture. Like most television towers, it is built of reinforced concrete and rises up like a rocket on the launching pad. The pierced conical

base seems to carry its mighty burden with effortless ease, although the tower is not static but constantly swaying—by up to 23 feet at the tip of the aerial.

This improbably high tower is rhythmically articulated only by the "rings," in which there are rooms for technical equipment, and, at a height of over 1,000 feet, by three observation platforms and a three-floor restaurant for 300 guests. Dimensions such as these call for new and still unfamiliar artistic standards, but they also convey a new feeling for distance and size in the cosmic age reflected in its architecture.

BERLIN, TELEVISION TOWER

Near Alexanderplatz in Berlin is the highest building in the GDR, the almost 1,200-foot-high television tower which was erected in reinforced concrete in 1966–69. The smooth and stark "needle" of the tower, soaring up on high, has a steel skeleton sphere more than halfway up as an aesthetically effective counterweight. It is 104 feet in diameter and is covered with a light-alloy skin having a facet surface.

The eight floors of the "globe" accommodate not only transmitting equipment but also the observation terrace. As a special attraction above this, at a height of nearly 680 feet, is the revolving café, which turns through 360° in one hour and gives a panorama of the whole city. Technical achievement and new artistic principles, such as the amalgam of the dominant needlelike thrust and the "floating" sphere—the silvery shimmer and charm of the structured ornamentation on the globe contrasting with the gray of the concrete shaft—are, in our epoch, factors of tower design which are contingent on and supplementary to each other.